A Time to Pray

D0130154

A TIME TO PRAY

365 Classic Prayers
to help you through the year

Compiled by Philip Law
Foreword by David Adam

A LION BOOK

This edition copyright © 1997 Lion Publishing

Published by
Lion Publishing plc
Mayfield House, 256 Banbury Road,
Oxford OX2 7DH, England
www.lion-publishing.co.uk
ISBN 0 7459 5112 0

First paperback edition 1997
First hardback edition 2002
10 9 8 7 6 5 4 3 2 1 0

A catalogue record for this book is available
from the British Library

Printed and bound in Great Britain by
Cox & Wyman Ltd, Reading, Berkshire

CONTENTS

FOREWORD

H ere is an opportunity to take a journey in time that will change your life. You will travel more than two thousand years in the space of one year of your life. You will meet great characters from the past and discover people who have shared in similar joys and sorrows, people who have plumbed depths and scaled heights, just as we do today. Here, through prayer, is offered a way to enrich your life and your sensitivity. This is a journey giving an opportunity to explore reality; and more, to encounter a deeper reality than you have known before. You will be given the opportunity to penetrate through the fantasies that the world weaves about you, to the ultimate reality.

To pray is to take part in a great exploration, to journey in depth as well as time. We will journey inwards to our innermost being, we will also look at the mysteries and wonders of the world in which we live until we come before that Great Majesty that fills us with awe. Through prayer we will open ourselves not only to God but to a new sensitivity towards each other. We will have the chance to discover that the Great Other comes to us in the other person that we meet today.

Prayer is truly meant to be a love affair between ourselves and the Beloved. It is so important that we use our own words and our own expressions to express our love. But, as we can discover, a wonderful poem will speak to a loved one, or a flower from a garden, so here we can find words that will enrich our relationship and our love. Here are prayers to increase our awareness, to tune our senses, to open our hearts. Here we can discover wonder upon wonder, and treasure upon treasure. Here attitudes, thought patterns and images can all be enriched. The wealth contained in these pages can alter our lives forever. We can use these prayers to enter into a stillness that is vibrant with the Presence and with all that comes to us.

To continue in such an adventure we need the guidance of those who have travelled this road before us, and so we look to the prayers of the past. The journey in time will take us from the Psalms in January to the Old and New Testament in February. Great prayers from the Early Fathers will enrich us in March, as will the Celtic prayers of April. In May we meet medieval Christians and move on to the saints, mystics and poets in June and July. A great wealth of prayer is being offered to us as we travel on through the Reformed Tradition to nineteenth-century Christians in August and September. In the last quarter, we move towards today with great hymn writers, twentieth-century Christians, and those who are our contemporaries. In these pages are some of the deepest thoughts and expressions of people who have gone before us. Prayers from the past resonate today because we share a common humanity, common dreams and hopes, common fears and joys. The experience of a fellow human who lived in the first millennium can guide us and enrich us as we approach the third millennium. Whatever our commitment we can be enriched by the Jew, the Catholic, the Orthodox or the Protestant, by those with a sure faith and by those who are seekers.

It is good that there are some restrictions. Do not go rushing from prayer to prayer; keep to one for the day, learn it, ponder it and make it your own. Let the prayer for the day speak throughout the day. When special events or feelings arise, use the index and share your thoughts with those who have gone before. Let the book last at least a year and enrich you day by day.

David Adam

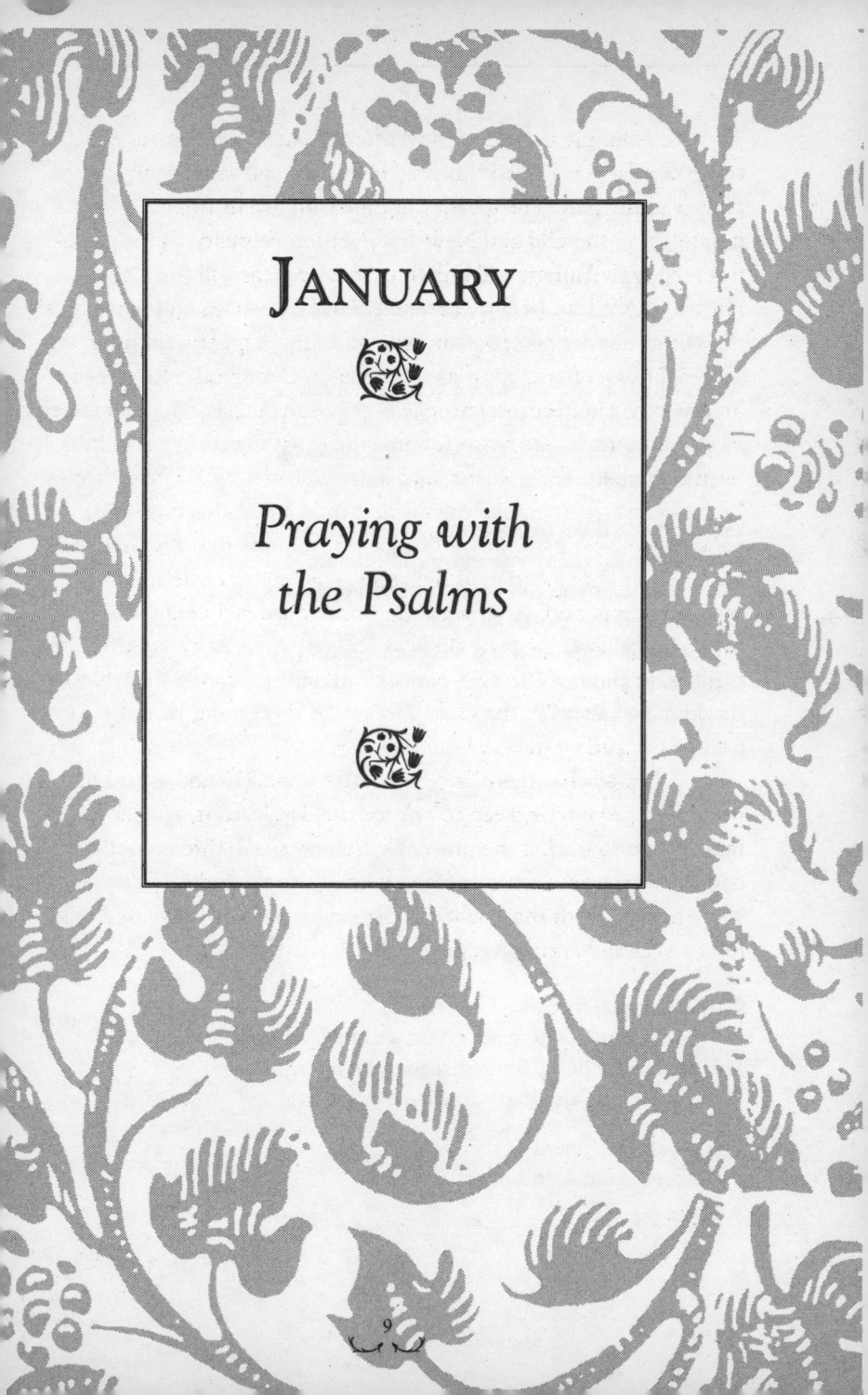

JANUARY

*Praying with
the Psalms*

🔹 JANUARY 1 🔹

O Lord, our Lord,
  your greatness is seen in all the world!
Your praise reaches up to the heavens;
  it is sung by children and babies.
You are safe and secure from all your enemies;
  you stop anyone who opposes you.

When I look at the sky, which you have made,
  at the moon and the stars, which you set in their places—
what are human beings, that you think of them;
  mere mortals, that you care for them?

Yet you made them inferior only to yourself;
  you crowned them with glory and honour.
You appointed them rulers over everything you made;
  you placed them over all creation:
  sheep and cattle, and the wild animals too;
  the birds and the fish
  and the creatures in the seas.

O Lord, our Lord,
  your greatness is seen in all the world!

Psalm 8

🔹 JANUARY 2 🔹

Why are you so far away, O Lord?
  Why do you hide yourself when we are in trouble?
The wicked are proud and persecute the poor;
  catch them in the traps they have made.

The wicked are proud of their evil desires;
  the greedy curse and reject the Lord...

O Lord, punish those wicked people!
    Remember those who are suffering!
How can the wicked despise God
    and say to themselves, 'He will not punish me'?

But you do see; you take notice of trouble and suffering
    and are always ready to help.
The helpless commit themselves to you;
    you have always helped the needy...

You will listen, O Lord, to the prayers of the lowly;
    you will give them courage.
You will hear the cries of the oppressed and the orphans;
    you will judge in their favour,
    so that mortal men may cause terror no more.

Psalm 10:1–3, 12–14, 17–18

❋ JANUARY 3 ❋

O Lord, who shall sojourn in thy tent?
    Who shall dwell on thy holy hill?

He who walks blamelessly, and does what is right,
    and speaks truth from his heart;
who does not slander with his tongue,
    and does no evil to his friend,
nor takes up a reproach against his neighbour;
    in whose eyes a reprobate is despised,
but who honours those who fear the Lord;
    who swears to his own hurt and does not change;
who does not put out his money at interest,
    and does not take a bribe against the innocent.

He who does these things shall never be moved.

Psalm 15

JANUARY 4

You, Lord, are all I have,
    and you give me all I need;
    my future is in your hands.
How wonderful are your gifts to me;
    how good they are!

I praise the Lord, because he guides me,
    and in the night my conscience warns me.
I am always aware of the Lord's presence;
    he is near, and nothing can shake me.

And so I am thankful and glad,
    and I feel completely secure,
    because you protect me from the power of death.
I have served you faithfully,
    and you will not abandon me to the world of the dead.

You will show me the path that leads to life;
    your presence fills me with joy
    and brings me pleasure for ever.

Psalm 16:5–11

JANUARY 5

The heavens are telling the glory of God;
    and the firmament proclaims his handiwork.
Day to day pours forth speech,
    and night to night declares knowledge.
There is no speech, nor are there words;
    their voice is not heard;
yet their voice goes out through all the earth,
    and their words to the end of the world.

In the heavens he has set a tent for the sun,
    which comes out like a bridegroom from his wedding canopy,
    and like a strong man runs its course with joy.

Its rising is from the end of the heavens,
　　and its circuit to the end of them;
　　and nothing is hidden from its heat.

The law of the Lord is perfect,
　　reviving the soul;
the decrees of the Lord are sure,
　　making wise the simple;
the precepts of the Lord are right,
　　rejoicing the heart;
the commandment of the Lord is clear,
　　enlightening the eyes;
the fear of the Lord is pure,
　　enduring for ever;
the ordinances of the Lord are true
　　and righteous altogether.
More to be desired are they than gold,
　　even much fine gold;
sweeter also than honey,
　　and drippings of the honeycomb...

Let the words of my mouth and the meditation of my heart
　　be acceptable to you,
　　O Lord, my rock and my redeemer.

Psalm 19:1–10, 14

❀ JANUARY 6 ❀

My God, my God, why have you forsaken me?
　　Why are you so far from helping me, from the words of my groaning?
O my God, I cry by day, but you do not answer;
　　and by night, but find no rest...

Yet it was you who took me from the womb;
　　you kept me safe on my mother's breast.
On you I was cast from my birth,
　　and since my mother bore me you have been my God.

Do not be far from me,
for trouble is near
and there is no one to help.

Psalm 22:1–2, 9–11

❧ JANUARY 7 ❧

The Lord is my shepherd;
I shall not want.
He maketh me to lie down in green pastures:
he leadeth me beside the still waters.
He restoreth my soul:
he leadeth me in the paths of righteousness
for his name's sake.
Yea, though I walk through the valley of the shadow of death,
I will fear no evil:
for thou art with me;
thy rod and thy staff they comfort me.

Thou preparest a table before me
in the presence of mine enemies:
thou anointest my head with oil;
my cup runneth over.
Surely goodness and mercy shall follow me all the days of my life:
and I will dwell in the house of the Lord for ever.

Psalm 23

❧ JANUARY 8 ❧

Teach me your ways, O Lord;
make them known to me.
Teach me to live according to your truth,
for you are my God, who saves me.
I always trust in you.

Remember, O Lord, your kindness and constant love
   which you have shown from long ago.
Forgive the sins and errors of my youth.
In your constant love and goodness,
   remember me, Lord!

Because the Lord is righteous and good,
   he teaches sinners the path they should follow.
He leads the humble in the right way
   and teaches them his will...

Turn to me, Lord, and be merciful to me,
   because I am lonely and weak.
Relieve me of my worries
   and save me from all my troubles.
Consider my distress and suffering
   and forgive all my sins.

Psalm 25:4–9, 16–18

🌸 JANUARY 9 🌸

Happy are those whose transgression is forgiven,
   whose sin is covered.
Happy are those to whom the Lord imputes no iniquity,
   and in whose spirit there is no deceit.

While I kept silence, my body wasted away
   through my groaning all day long.
For day and night your hand was heavy upon me;
   my strength was dried up as by the heat of summer.

Then I acknowledged my sin to you,
   and I did not hide my iniquity;
I said, 'I will confess my transgressions to the Lord,'
   and you forgave the guilt of my sin.

Therefore let all who are faithful
   offer prayer to you;

at a time of distress, the rush of mighty waters
    shall not reach them.
You are a hiding-place for me;
    you preserve me from trouble;
    you surround me with glad cries of deliverance.

Psalm 32:1–7

❦ JANUARY 10 ❦

Thy mercy, O Lord, is in the heavens;
    and thy faithfulness reacheth unto the clouds.
Thy righteousness is like the great mountains;
    thy judgments are a great deep:
    O Lord, thou preservest man and beast.

How excellent is thy lovingkindness, O God!
    therefore the children of men put their trust
    under the shadow of thy wings.
They shall be abundantly satisfied with the fatness of thy house;
    and thou shalt make them drink of the river of thy pleasures.
For with thee is the fountain of life:
    in thy light shall we see light.

Psalm 36:5–9

❦ JANUARY 11 ❦

Do not be vexed because of evildoers
    or envy those who do wrong.
For like the grass they soon wither,
    and like green pasture they fade away.

Trust in the Lord and do good;
    settle in the land and find safe pasture.
Delight in the Lord,
    and he will grant you your heart's desire.
Commit your way to the Lord;
    trust in him, and he will act.

He will make your righteousness shine clear as the day
   and the justice of your cause like the brightness of noon.

Wait quietly for the Lord, be patient till he comes;
   do not envy those who gain their ends,
   or be vexed at their success.

Be angry no more, have done with wrath;
   do not be vexed: that leads to evil.

Psalm 37:1–8

❁ JANUARY 12 ❁

I said, 'I will guard my ways
   that I may not sin with my tongue;
I will keep a muzzle on my mouth
   as long as the wicked are in my presence.'
I was silent and still;
   I held my peace to no avail;
my distress grew worse,
   my heart became hot within me.
While I mused, the fire burned;
   then I spoke with my tongue:

'Lord, let me know my end,
   and what is the measure of my days;
   let me know how fleeting my life is.
You have made my days a few handbreadths,
   and my lifetime is as nothing in your sight.
Surely everyone stands as a mere breath.
Surely everyone goes about like a shadow.
Surely for nothing they are in turmoil;
   they heap up, and do not know who will gather...

'Hear my prayer, O Lord,
   and give ear to my cry;
   do not hold your peace at my tears.

For I am your passing guest,
　　an alien, like all my forebears.
Turn your gaze away from me, that I may smile again,
　　before I depart and am no more.'

Psalm 39:1–6, 12–13

❀ JANUARY 13 ❀

As a deer longs for flowing streams,
　　so my soul longs for you, O God.
My soul thirsts for God,
　　for the living God.
When shall I come and behold
　　the face of God?...

Deep calls to deep
　　at the thunder of your cataracts;
all your waves and your billows
　　have gone over me.
By day the Lord commands his steadfast love,
　　and at night his song is with me,
　　a prayer to the God of my life.

I say to God, my rock,
　　'Why have you forgotten me?
Why must I walk about mournfully
　　because the enemy oppresses me?'
As with a deadly wound in my body,
　　my adversaries taunt me,
while they say to me continually,
　　'Where is your God?'

Why are you cast down, O my soul,
　　and why are you disquieted within me?
Hope in God; for I shall again praise him,
　　my help and my God.

Psalm 42:1–2, 7–11

They that trust in their wealth,
    and boast themselves in the multitude of their riches;
None of them can by any means redeem his brother,
    nor give to God a ransom for him:
(For the redemption of their soul is precious,
    and it ceaseth for ever:)
That he should still live for ever,
    and not see corruption.

For he seeth that wise men die,
    likewise the fool and the brutish person perish,
    and leave their wealth to others.
Their inward thought is, that their houses shall continue for ever,
    and their dwelling places to all generations;
    they call their lands after their own names.

Nevertheless man being in honour abideth not:
    he is like the beasts that perish.

This their way is their folly:
    yet their posterity approve their sayings.
Like sheep they are laid in the grave;
    death shall feed on them;
and the upright shall have dominion over them in the morning;
    and their beauty shall consume in the grave from their dwelling.
But God will redeem my soul from the power of the grave:
    for he shall receive me.

Psalm 49:6–15

🌸 JANUARY 15 🌸

Have mercy on me, O God, in your faithful love,
    in your great tenderness wipe away my offences;
wash me clean from my guilt,
    purify me from my sin.

For I am well aware of my offences,
my sin is constantly in mind.
Against you, you alone, I have sinned,
I have done what you see to be wrong…

God, create in me a clean heart,
renew within me a resolute spirit,
do not thrust me away from your presence,
do not take away from me your spirit of holiness.

Give me back the joy of your salvation,
sustain in me a generous spirit.

Psalm 51:1–4, 10–12

January 16

God, you are my God, I pine for you;
my heart thirsts for you,
my body longs for you,
as a land parched, dreary and waterless.
Thus have I gazed on you in the sanctuary,
seeing your power and your glory.

Better your faithful love than life itself;
my lips will praise you.
Thus I will bless you all my life,
in your name lift up my hands.
All my longings fulfilled as with fat and rich foods,
a song of joy on my lips and praise in my mouth.

On my bed when I think of you,
I muse on you in the watches of the night,
for you have always been my help;
in the shadow of your wings I rejoice;
my heart clings to you,
your right hand supports me.

Psalm 63:1–8

❧ JANUARY 17 ❧

God, endow the king with your own fair judgment,
  the son of the king with your own saving justice,
that he may rule your people with justice,
  and your poor with fair judgment.

Mountains and hills,
  bring peace to the people!
With justice he will judge the poor of the people,
  he will save the children of the needy
  and crush their oppressors.

In the sight of the sun and the moon he will endure,
  age after age.
He will come down like rain on mown grass,
  like showers moistening the land:

In his days uprightness shall flourish,
  and peace in plenty till the moon is no more...

May his name be blessed for ever,
  and endure in the sight of the sun.
In him shall be blessed every race in the world,
  and all nations call him blessed.

Psalm 72: 1–7, 17

❧ JANUARY 18 ❧

My feet had almost slipped,
  my foothold had all but given way,
because boasters roused my envy
  when I saw how the wicked prosper.
No painful suffering for them!
  They are sleek and sound in body;
they are not in trouble like ordinary mortals,
  nor are they afflicted like other folk.

Therefore they wear pride like a necklace
  and violence like a robe that wraps them round.
Their eyes gleam through folds of fat,
  while vain fancies flit through their minds.
Their talk is all mockery and malice;
  high-handedly they threaten oppression.
Their slanders reach up to heaven,
  while their tongues are never still on earth…

I set my mind to understand this
  but I found it too hard for me,
until I went into God's sanctuary,
  where I saw clearly what their destiny would be.

Indeed you place them on slippery ground
  and drive them headlong into utter ruin!
In a moment they are destroyed,
  disasters making an end of them,
like a dream when one awakes, Lord,
  like images dismissed when one rouses from sleep!

My mind was embittered,
  and I was pierced to the heart.
I was too brutish to understand,
  in your sight, God, no better than a beast.
Yet I am always with you;
  you hold my right hand.
You guide me by your counsel
  and afterwards you will receive me with glory.
Whom have I in heaven but you?
  And having you, I desire nothing else on earth.
Though heart and body fail,
  yet God is the rock of my heart, my portion for ever.

Psalm 73:2–9,16–26

❧ JANUARY 19 ❧

Bow down thine ear, O Lord, hear me:
    for I am poor and needy.
    Preserve my soul; for I am holy:
O thou my God, save thy servant that trusteth in thee.
    Be merciful unto me, O Lord:
    for I cry unto thee daily.
Rejoice the soul of thy servant:
    for unto thee, O Lord, do I lift up my soul.
For thou, Lord, art good, and ready to forgive;
    and plenteous in mercy unto all them that call upon thee.
Give ear, O Lord, unto my prayer;
    and attend to the voice of my supplications.
In the day of my trouble I will call upon thee:
    for thou wilt answer me.

Among the gods there is none like unto thee, O Lord;
    neither are there any works like unto thy works.
All nations whom thou hast made
    shall come and worship before thee, O Lord;
    and shall glorify thy name.
For thou art great, and doest wondrous things:
    thou art God alone.

Teach me thy way, O Lord;
    I will walk in thy truth:
    unite my heart to fear thy name.
I will praise thee, O Lord my God, with all my heart:
    and I will glorify thy name for evermore.

Psalm 86:1–12

Lord, thou hast been our dwelling place
    in all generations.
Before the mountains were brought forth,
    or ever thou hadst formed the earth and the world,
even from everlasting to everlasting,
    thou art God.

Thou turnest man to destruction;
    and sayest, Return, ye children of men.
For a thousand years in thy sight
    are but as yesterday when it is past,
    and as a watch in the night.
Thou carriest them away as with a flood; they are as a sleep:
    in the morning they are like grass which groweth up.
In the morning it flourisheth, and groweth up;
    in the evening it is cut down, and withereth.
For we are consumed by thine anger,
    and by thy wrath are we troubled.
Thou hast set our iniquities before thee,
    our secret sins in the light of thy countenance.
For all our days are passed away in thy wrath:
    we spend our years as a tale that is told.
The days of our years are threescore years and ten;
    and if by reason of strength they be fourscore years,
yet is their strength labour and sorrow;
    for it is soon cut off, and we fly away.
Who knoweth the power of thine anger?
    even according to thy fear, so is thy wrath.
So teach us to number our days,
    that we may apply our hearts unto wisdom.

Psalm 90:1–12

O sing to the Lord a new song;
   sing to the Lord, all the earth.
Sing to the Lord, bless his name;
   tell of his salvation from day to day.
Declare his glory among the nations,
   his marvellous works among all the peoples.
For great is the Lord, and greatly to be praised;
   he is to be revered above all gods.
For all the gods of the peoples are idols,
   but the Lord made the heavens.
Honour and majesty are before him;
   strength and beauty are in his sanctuary.
Ascribe to the Lord, O families of the peoples,
   ascribe to the Lord glory and strength.
Ascribe to the Lord the glory due his name;
   bring an offering, and come into his courts.
Worship the Lord in holy splendour;
   tremble before him, all the earth.

Say among the nations, 'The Lord is king!
   The world is firmly established; it shall never be moved.
   He will judge the peoples with equity.'
Let the heavens be glad, and let the earth rejoice;
   let the sea roar, and all that fills it;
   let the field exult, and everything in it.
Then shall all the trees of the forest sing for joy
   before the Lord; for he is coming,
   for he is coming to judge the earth.
He will judge the world with righteousness,
   and the peoples with his truth.

Psalm 96:1–13

Hear my prayer, O Lord;
    let my cry come to thee!
Do not hide thy face from me
    in the day of my distress!
Incline thy ear to me;
    answer me speedily in the day when I call!

For my days pass away like smoke,
    and my bones burn like a furnace.
My heart is smitten like grass, and withered;
    I forgot to eat my bread.
Because of my loud groaning
    my bones cleave to my flesh.
I am like a vulture of the wilderness,
    like an owl of the waste places;
I lie awake,
    I am like a lonely bird on the housetop...
My days are like an evening shadow;
    I wither away like grass.

But thou, O Lord, art enthroned for ever;
    thy name endures to all generations...

Of old thou didst lay the foundation of the earth,
    and the heavens are the work of thy hands.
They will perish, but thou dost endure;
    they will all wear out like a garment.
Thou changest them like raiment, and they pass away;
    but thou art the same, and thy years have no end.
The children of thy servants shall dwell secure;
    their posterity shall be established before thee.

Psalm 102:1–7, 11–12, 25–28

Bless the Lord, O my soul:
    and all that is within me, bless his holy name.
Bless the Lord, O my soul,
    and forget not all his benefits:
Who forgiveth all thine iniquities;
    who healeth all thy diseases;
Who redeemeth thy life from destruction;
    who crowneth thee with lovingkindness and tender mercies;
Who satisfieth thy mouth with good things;
    so that thy youth is renewed like the eagle's.

The Lord executeth righteousness
    and judgment for all that are oppressed.

He made known his ways unto Moses,
    his acts unto the children of Israel.
The Lord is merciful and gracious,
    slow to anger, and plenteous in mercy.
He will not always chide:
    neither will he keep his anger for ever.
He hath not dealt with us after our sins;
    nor rewarded us according to our iniquities.
For as the heaven is high above the earth,
    so great is his mercy toward them that fear him.
As far as the east is from the west,
    so far hath he removed our transgressions from us.
Like as a father pitieth his children,
    so the Lord pitieth them that fear him.
For he knoweth our frame;
    he remembereth that we are dust.
As for man, his days are as grass:
    as a flower of the field, so he flourisheth.
For the wind passeth over it, and it is gone;
    and the place thereof shall know it no more.
But the mercy of the Lord
    is from everlasting to everlasting upon them that fear him,
    and his righteousness unto children's children;

To such as keep his covenant,
and to those that remember his commandments to do them.

The Lord hath prepared his throne in the heavens;
and his kingdom ruleth over all.

Bless the Lord, ye his angels, that excel in strength,
that do his commandments,
hearkening unto the voice of his word.
Bless ye the Lord, all ye his hosts;
ye ministers of his, that do his pleasure.
Bless the Lord, all his works in all places of his dominion:
bless the Lord, O my soul.

Psalm 103

🍀 JANUARY 24 🍀

Bless the Lord, O my soul.

O Lord my God, thou art very great;
thou art clothed with honour and majesty.
Who coverest thyself with light as with a garment:
who stretchest out the heavens like a curtain:
Who layeth the beams of his chambers in the waters:
who maketh the clouds his chariot:
who walketh upon the wings of the wind:
Who maketh his angels spirits;
his ministers a flaming fire:

Who laid the foundations of the earth,
that it should not be removed for ever.
Thou coveredst it with the deep as with a garment:
the waters stood above the mountains.
At thy rebuke they fled;
at the voice of thy thunder they hasted away.
They go up by the mountains;
they go down by the valleys
unto the place which thou hast founded for them.

Thou hast set a bound that they may not pass over;
    that they turn not again to cover the earth.

He sendeth the springs into the valleys,
    which run among the hills.
They give drink to every beast of the field:
    the wild asses quench their thirst.
By them shall the fowls of the heaven have their habitation,
    which sing among the branches.
He watereth the hills from his chambers:
    the earth is satisfied with the fruit of thy works.

He causeth the grass to grow for the cattle,
    and herb for the service of man:
    that he may bring forth food out of the earth;
And wine that maketh glad the heart of man...

Thou makest darkness, and it is night:
    wherein all the beasts of the forest do creep forth.
The young lions roar after their prey,
    and seek their meat from God.
The sun ariseth, they gather themselves together,
    and lay them down in their dens.
Man goeth forth unto his work
    and to his labour until the evening.

O Lord, how manifold are thy works!
    in wisdom hast thou made them all:
    the earth is full of thy riches.
So is this great and wide sea,
    wherein are things creeping innumerable,
    both small and great beasts.
There go the ships:
    there is that leviathan,
    whom thou hast made to play therein.

These wait all upon thee;
    that thou mayest give them their meat in due season.
That thou givest them they gather:
    thou openest thine hand, they are filled with good.

Thou hidest thy face, they are troubled:
 thou takest away their breath, they die,
 and return to their dust.
Thou sendest forth thy spirit, they are created:
 and thou renewest the face of the earth.

Psalm 104:1–15, 20–30

🌸 JANUARY 25 🌸

Praise the Lord.

With all my heart I shall give thanks to the Lord
 in the congregation, in the assembly of the upright.
Great are the works of the Lord,
 pondered over by all who delight in them.
His deeds are full of majesty and splendour;
 his righteousness stands sure for ever…
His works are truth and justice;
 all his precepts are trustworthy,
established to endure for ever,
 enacted in faithfulness and truth.
He sent and redeemed his people;
 he decreed that his covenant should endure for ever.
 Holy and awe-inspiring is his name.
The fear of the Lord is the beginning of wisdom,
 and they who live by it grow in understanding.
 Praise will be his for ever.

Psalm 111:1–3, 7–10

🌸 JANUARY 26 🌸

Teach me, O Lord, to follow your decrees;
 then I will keep them to the end.
Give me understanding, and I will keep your law
 and obey it with all my heart.

Direct me in the path of your commands,
    for there I find delight.
Turn my heart towards your statutes
    and not towards selfish gain.
Turn my eyes away from worthless things;
    preserve my life according to your word...

How sweet are your words to my taste,
    sweeter than honey to my mouth!
I gain understanding from your precepts;
    therefore I hate every wrong path.

Your word is a lamp to my feet
    and a light for my path.
I have taken an oath and confirmed it,
    that I will follow your righteous laws.
I have suffered much;
    preserve my life, O Lord, according to your word.
Accept, O Lord, the willing praise of my mouth,
    and teach me your laws...
Your statutes are my heritage for ever;
    they are the joy of my heart.
My heart is set on keeping your decrees
    to the very end.

Psalm 119:33–37, 103–108, 111–12

🏵 JANUARY 27 🏵

Lord, I have given up my pride
    and turned away from my arrogance.
I am not concerned with great matters
    or with subjects too difficult for me.
    Instead, I am content and at peace.
As a child lies quietly in its mother's arms,
    so my heart is quiet within me.

Psalm 131:1–2

O Lord, thou hast searched me, and known me.
Thou knowest my downsitting and mine uprising,
   thou understandest my thought afar off.
Thou compassest my path and my lying down,
   and art acquainted with all my ways.
For there is not a word in my tongue,
   but, lo, O Lord, thou knowest it altogether.
Thou hast beset me behind and before,
   and laid thine hand upon me.
Such knowledge is too wonderful for me;
   it is high, I cannot attain unto it.

Whither shall I go from thy spirit?
   or whither shall I flee from thy presence?
If I ascend up into heaven, thou art there:
   if I make my bed in hell, behold, thou art there.
If I take the wings of the morning,
   and dwell in the uttermost parts of the sea;
Even there shall thy hand lead me,
   and thy right hand shall hold me.
If I say, Surely the darkness shall cover me;
   even the night shall be light about me.
Yea, the darkness hideth not from thee;
   but the night shineth as the day:
   the darkness and the light are both alike to thee.
For thou hast possessed my reins:
   thou hast covered me in my mother's womb.
I will praise thee; for I am fearfully and wonderfully made:
   marvellous are thy works;
   and that my soul knoweth right well.
My substance was not hid from thee,
   when I was made in secret,
   and curiously wrought in the lowest parts of the earth.
Thine eyes did see my substance, yet being unperfect;
   and in thy book all my members were written,

which in continuance were fashioned,
　　when as yet there was none of them.
How precious also are thy thoughts unto me, O God!
　　how great is the sum of them!
If I should count them, they are more in number than the sand:
　　when I awake, I am still with thee.

Psalm 139:1–18

❧ JANUARY 29 ❧

Lord, I call to you, come to my aid quickly;
　　listen to me when I call.
May my prayer be like incense set before you,
　　the lifting up of my hands like the evening offering.

Lord, set a guard on my mouth;
　　keep watch at the door of my lips.
Let not my thoughts incline to evil,
　　to the pursuit of evil courses
with those who are evildoers;
　　let me not partake of their delights.

I would rather be beaten by the righteous
　　and reproved by those who are good.
My head will not be anointed with the oil of the wicked,
　　for while I live my prayer is against their wickedness.

Psalm 141:1–5

❧ JANUARY 30 ❧

I will extol thee, my God, O king;
　　and I will bless thy name for ever and ever.
Every day will I bless thee;
　　and I will praise thy name for ever and ever.
Great is the Lord, and greatly to be praised;
　　and his greatness is unsearchable.

One generation shall praise thy works to another,
and shall declare thy mighty acts.
I will speak of the glorious honour of thy majesty,
and of thy wondrous works.
And men shall speak of the might of thy terrible acts:
and I will declare thy greatness.
They shall abundantly utter the memory of thy great goodness,
and shall sing of thy righteousness.

The Lord is gracious, and full of compassion;
slow to anger, and of great mercy.
The Lord is good to all:
and his tender mercies are over all his works.

All thy works shall praise thee, O Lord;
and thy saints shall bless thee.
They shall speak of the glory of thy kingdom,
and talk of thy power;
To make known to the sons of men his mighty acts,
and the glorious majesty of his kingdom.
Thy kingdom is an everlasting kingdom,
and thy dominion endureth throughout all generations...

The Lord is nigh unto all them that call upon him,
to all that call upon him in truth.
He will fulfil the desire of them that fear him:
he also will hear their cry, and will save them.
The Lord preserveth all them that love him:
but all the wicked will he destroy.

My mouth shall speak the praise of the Lord:
and let all flesh bless his holy name for ever and ever.

Psalm 145:1–13, 18–21

Praise the Lord.

Praise the Lord from the heavens,
    praise him in the heights above.
Praise him, all his angels,
    praise him, all his heavenly hosts.
Praise him, sun and moon,
    praise him, all you shining stars.
Praise him, you highest heavens
    and you waters above the skies.
Let them praise the name of the Lord,
    for he commanded and they were created.
He set them in place for ever and ever;
    he gave a decree that will never pass away.

Praise the Lord from the earth,
    you great sea creatures and all ocean depths,
lightning and hail, snow and clouds,
    stormy winds that do his bidding,
you mountains and all hills,
    fruit trees and all cedars,
wild animals and all cattle,
    small creatures and flying birds,
kings of the earth and all nations,
    you princes and all rulers on earth,
young men and maidens,
    old men and children.

Let them praise the name of the Lord,
    for his name alone is exalted;
    his splendour is above the earth and the heavens.

Psalm 148:1–13

FEBRUARY

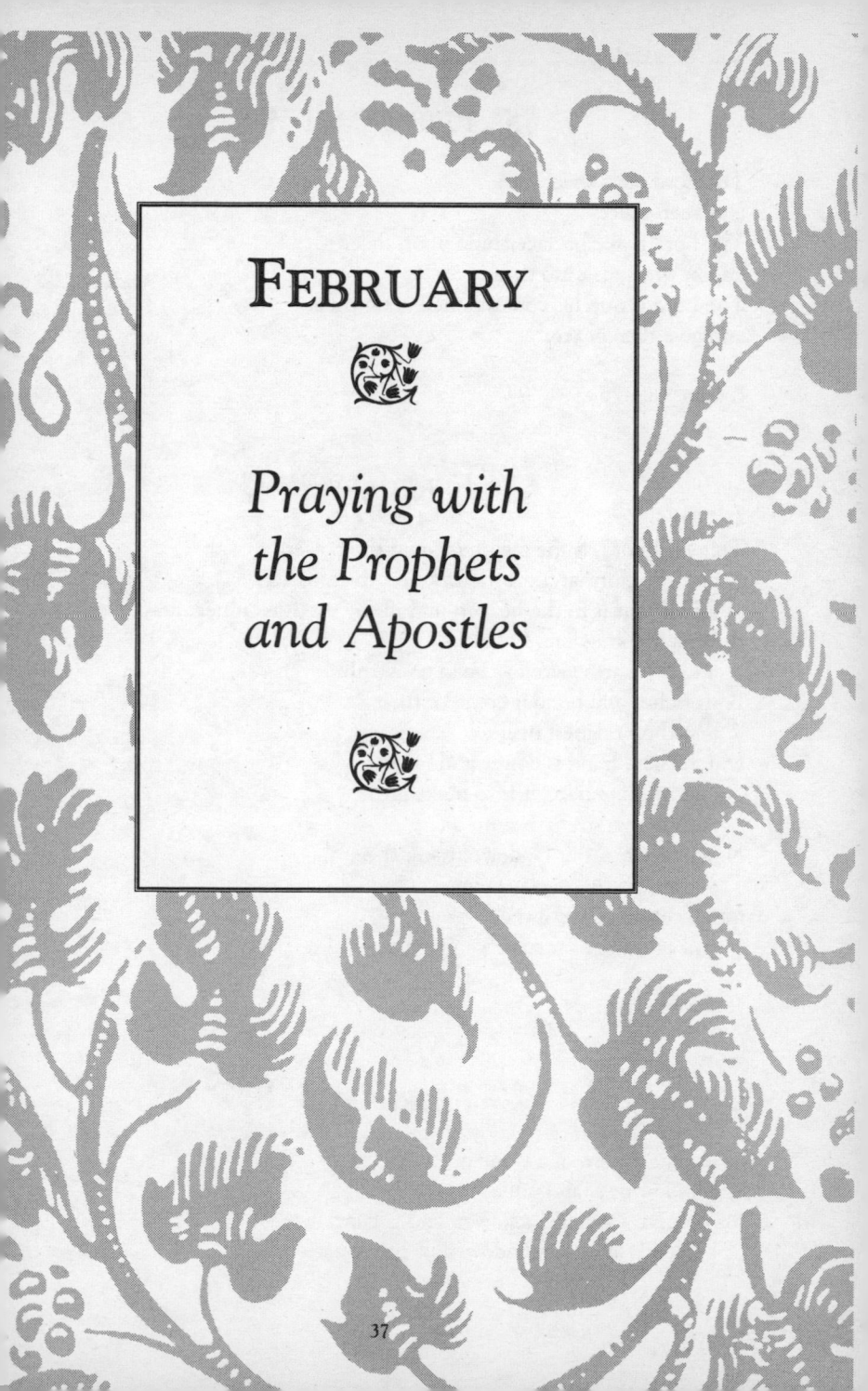

*Praying with
the Prophets
and Apostles*

❦ FEBRUARY 1 ❦

The Lord bless thee,
and keep thee:
The Lord make his face shine upon thee,
and be gracious unto thee:
The Lord lift up his countenance upon thee,
and give thee peace.

Numbers 6:24–26

❦ FEBRUARY 2 ❦

Thine, O Lord, is the greatness, and the power,
   and the glory, and the victory, and the majesty:
   for all that is in the heaven and in the earth is thine;
thine is the kingdom, O Lord,
   and thou art exalted as head above all.
Both riches and honour come of thee,
   and thou reignest over all;
and in thine hand is power and might;
   and in thine hand it is to make great,
   and to give strength unto all.
Now therefore, our God, we thank thee,
   and praise thy glorious name…
for all things come of thee,
   and of thine own have we given thee.

1 Chronicles 29:11–14

❦ FEBRUARY 3 ❦

Man that is born of a woman
   is of few days and full of trouble.
He cometh forth like a flower, and is cut down:
   he fleeth also as a shadow, and continueth not.

And doth thou open thine eyes upon such an one,
and bringest me into judgment with thee?...

For there is hope of a tree, if it be cut down,
that it will sprout again,
and that the tender branch thereof will not cease.
Though the root thereof wax old in the earth,
and the stock thereof die in the ground;
Yet through the scent of water it will bud,
and bring forth boughs like a plant.
But man dieth, and wasteth away:
yea, man giveth up the ghost, and where is he?
As the waters fail from the sea,
and the flood decayeth and drieth up:
So man lieth down, and riseth not:
till the heavens be no more, they shall not awake,
nor be raised out of their sleep.

O that thou wouldest hide me in the grave,
that thou wouldest keep me secret, until thy wrath be past,
that thou wouldest appoint me a set time,
and remember me!
If a man die, shall he live again?
all the days of my appointed time will I wait,
till my change come.
Thou shalt call, and I will answer thee:
thou wilt have a desire to the work of thine hands.

Job 14:1–3, 7–15

FEBRUARY 4

God of all wisdom
Help me to think before I speak,
before I make rash promises.
For you are in heaven and I am on earth,
so I will say no more than I have to.
Help me to realize that the more I talk,
the more likely I am to say something foolish.

So when I make a promise to you, O my God,
help me keep it as quickly as possible!

Based on Ecclesiastes 5:2–4

❀ FEBRUARY 5 ❀

Yahweh, you are my God,
   I shall praise you to the heights,
   I shall praise your name;
for you have accomplished marvels,
   plans long-conceived, faithfully, firmly…
Mighty peoples will honour you,
   the city of pitiless nations hold you in awe;
For you have been a refuge for the weak,
   a refuge for the needy in distress,
a shelter from the storm,
   shade from the heat;
for the breath of the pitiless
   is like a winter storm.
Like heat in a dry land you calm the foreigners' tumult;
   as heat under the shadow of a cloud,
   so the song of the pitiless dies away.

Isaiah 25:1, 3–5

❀ FEBRUARY 6 ❀

Lord, I will live for you, for you alone;
   Heal me and let me live.
My bitterness will turn into peace.
   You save my life from all danger;
   You forgive all my sins.
No one in the world of the dead can praise you;
   The dead cannot trust in your faithfulness.
It is the living who praise you,
   As I praise you now.

Isaiah 38:16–19

You were despised and rejected by men,
  a man of sorrows, and familiar with suffering.
Like one from whom men hide their faces
  you were despised, and we esteemed you not.
Surely you took up our infirmities
  and carried our sorrows,
yet we considered you stricken by God,
  smitten by him, and afflicted.
But you were pierced for our transgressions,
  you were crushed for our iniquities;
the punishment that brought us peace was upon you,
  and by your wounds we are healed.
We all, like sheep, have gone astray,
  each of us has turned to his own way;
and the Lord has laid on you
  the iniquity of us all.

You were oppressed and afflicted,
  yet you did not open your mouth;
you were led like a lamb to the slaughter,
  and as a sheep before her shearers is silent,
  so you did not open your mouth...

Therefore God has given you a portion among the great,
  and you will divide the spoils with the strong,
because you poured out your life unto death,
  and were numbered with the transgressors.

Based on Isaiah 53:3–7, 12

❦ FEBRUARY 8 ❦

High and holy God,
who lives for ever,
who lives in a high and holy place,
but who also lives with us

if we are humble and repentant:
restore our confidence and hope,
give us life
and do not continue to accuse us;
do not be angry with us for ever.

You were angry with us
because of our sin and greed,
because we were stubborn
and kept going our own way;
but now you heal us and help us,
you comfort those who mourn,
you offer peace to all,
both near and far.

Based on Isaiah 57:15–19

🌼 FEBRUARY 9 🌼

Look down from heaven and see
    from your lofty throne, holy and glorious.
Where are your zeal and your might?
    Your tenderness and compassion are withheld from us.
But you are our Father...
    our Redeemer from of old is your name.
Why, O Lord, do you make us wander from your ways
and harden our hearts so that we do not revere you?...

Oh, that you would rend the heavens and come down,
    that the mountains would tremble before you!
As when fire sets twigs ablaze
    and causes water to boil,
come down to make your name known to your enemies
    and cause the nations to quake before you!...

All of us have become like one who is unclean,
    and all our righteous acts are like filthy rags;
we all shrivel up like a leaf,
    and like the wind our sins sweep us away.

No-one calls on your name
  or strives to lay hold of you;
for you have hidden your face from us
  and made us waste away because of our sins.

Yet, O Lord, you are our Father.
  We are the clay, you are the potter;
  we are all the work of your hand.
Do not be angry beyond measure, O Lord;
  do not remember our sins for ever.
Oh, look upon us we pray,
  for we are all your people.

Isaiah 63:15–17; 64:1–2, 6–9

❧ FEBRUARY 10 ❧

Ever since I was a child,
you loved me.
You called me;
but the more you called to me,
the more I turned away from you.
Yet you were the one who taught me to walk.
You took me up in your arms,
but I did not acknowledge that you took care of me.
You drew me to you with affection and love.
You picked me up and held me to your cheek.
You bent down to me and fed me.
Yet I insisted on turning away from you.
And now I cry out:
Do not give me up! Do not abandon me!
For you are God and not a human being.
I pray that you, the Holy One, will always be with me.

Based on Hosea 11:1–9

❦ FEBRUARY 11 ❦

Our Father in heaven,
    may your name be hallowed;
your kingdom come,
    your will be done,
    on earth as in heaven.
Give us today our daily bread.
Forgive us the wrong we have done,
    as we have forgiven those who have wronged us.
And do not put us to the test,
    but save us from the evil one.

Matthew 6:9–13

❦ FEBRUARY 12 ❦

Lord Jesus,
Let me not worry about the food and drink
    I need to stay alive,
    or about clothes for my body.
Help me to see that life is worth
    far more than food,
    and the body more than clothes.
Increase my faith in my Father in heaven
    who knows that I need all these things.
Increase my faith, that I may be concerned
    above everything else
    with his kingdom
    and with what he requires of me.

Based on Matthew 6:25, 32–33

❧ FEBRUARY 13 ❧

My soul magnifies you, my Lord,
  and my spirit rejoices in God my Saviour,
  for you have looked with favour on the lowliness of your servant.
You, the Mighty One, have done great things for me,
  and holy is your name.
Your mercy is for those who fear you from generation to generation.
You have scattered the proud in the thoughts of their hearts.
You have brought down the powerful from their thrones,
  and lifted up the lowly;
You have filled the hungry with good things,
  and sent the rich away empty.

Based on Luke 1:46–55

❧ FEBRUARY 14 ❧

Merciful God,
I offer myself as a living sacrifice;
I dedicate myself to your service.

Let me not conform to the standards of this world;
but transform me inwardly,
that I may know your will—
what is good and pleasing and perfect.

Let me not think of myself more highly than I should;
but let me be modest in my thinking,
and judge myself according to the amount of faith you have given me.

May my love be completely sincere;
may I hate what is evil,
and hold on to what is good.

May my hope keep me joyful;
may I be patient in troubles,
and pray at all times.

Help me to bless those who persecute me,
to be happy with those who are happy,
to weep with those who weep.

Help me to have the same concern for everyone,
to be humble and peaceful,
and never take revenge.

Let me not be defeated by evil;
but let me conquer evil with good.

Based on Romans 12:1–3, 9–21

❧ FEBRUARY 15 ❧

I pray for the gift of love;
   for if I have not love, I am nothing.
Teach me, in love, to be patient and kind;
   not envious, boastful or conceited.
Never let me be rude, selfish or quick to take offence;
   may I keep no score of wrongs.
Never let me take pleasure in the sins of others;
   may I take delight in the truth.
For then there will be nothing my love cannot face;
   no limit to its faith, its hope, its endurance.
My love will never end.

Based on 1 Corinthians 13:2, 4–8

❧ FEBRUARY 16 ❧

May the grace of the Lord Jesus Christ, and the love of God, and the
fellowship of the Holy Spirit be with us all, evermore.

Based on 2 Corinthians 13:14

❀ FEBRUARY 17 ❀

I pray that the God of our Lord Jesus Christ, the Father of glory, may give me a spirit of wisdom and revelation as I come to know him, so that, with the eyes of my heart enlightened, I may know what is the hope to which he has called me, what are the riches of his glorious inheritance among the saints, and what is the immeasurable greatness of his power for those who believe.

Based on Ephesians 1:17–19

❀ FEBRUARY 18 ❀

Father, I fall on my knees before you. I ask you from the wealth of your glory to give me power through your Spirit to be strong in my inner self. I pray that Christ will make his home in my heart, that I may have the power to understand how broad and long, how high and deep, is Christ's love. For by means of your power working in me you are able to do so much more than I can ever ask for, or even think of. To you, Father, be the glory in the church and in Christ Jesus for all time, for ever and ever! Amen.

Based on Ephesians 3:14–21

❀ FEBRUARY 19 ❀

Father, if I become angry, do not let my anger lead me into sin; do not let me use harmful words, but words that build up and do good to those who hear me; and do not let me make your Holy Spirit sad. Help me to get rid of all bitterness and hate; help me to be kind and tender-hearted; and help me to forgive, as you have forgiven me through Christ.

Based on Ephesians 4:26, 29–32

❦ FEBRUARY 20 ❦

I pray that your love will keep on growing more and more, together with true knowledge and perfect judgment, so that you will be able to choose what is best. Then you will be free from all impurity and blame on the Day of Christ. Your lives will be filled with the truly good qualities which only Jesus Christ can produce, for the glory and praise of God.

Philippians 1:9–11

❦ FEBRUARY 21 ❦

Lord Jesus Christ,
You always had the nature of God,
   but you did not try to remain equal with God.
Of your own free will you gave up all you had,
   and took the nature of a servant.
You became like a human being
   and appeared in human likeness.
You were humble and walked the path of obedience
   all the way to death—your death on the cross.
For this reason God raised you to the highest place above
   and gave you the name that is greater than any other name.
And so, in honour of your name, I fall on my knees,
   and openly proclaim that you are my Lord,
   to the glory of God the Father.

Based on Philippians 2:6–11

❦ FEBRUARY 22 ❦

Lord, give me your peace, even though it is far beyond my understanding. May it keep my heart in union with Christ. May it fill my mind with those things that are good and that deserve praise: things that are true, noble, right, pure, lovely, and honourable. Give me your peace, Lord, and may it always be with me.

Based on Philippians 4:7–9

❧ FEBRUARY 23 ❧

Gracious Father, I ask that through your perfect wisdom and spiritual understanding I may reach the fullest knowledge of your will, and so be able to lead a life worthy and acceptable to you in all its aspects: bearing fruit in every kind of good work and growing in spiritual knowledge; fortified, in accordance with your glorious strength, with all power always to persevere and endure; giving thanks with joy that you have made me able to share the lot of your holy people and with them to inherit the light. Because that is what you have done: you have rescued me from the ruling force of darkness and transferred me to the kingdom of your Son.

Based on Colossians 1:9–13

❧ FEBRUARY 24 ❧

May our Lord Jesus Christ himself and God our Father, who loved us and in his grace gave us unfailing courage and a firm hope, encourage you and strengthen you always to do and say what is good.

2 Thessalonians 2:16–17

❧ FEBRUARY 25 ❧

I thank you, O Christ, that you suffered for me,
leaving me an example, that I should follow in your steps.
You committed no sin, and no deceit was found in your mouth.
When you were abused, you did not return abuse;
when you suffered, you did not threaten;
but you entrusted yourself to the one who judges justly.
You yourself bore my sins in your body on the cross,
so that, free from sins, I might live for righteousness;
by your wounds I have been healed.
For I was like a lost sheep,
but now I have returned to the shepherd and guardian of my soul.

Based on 1 Peter 2:21–25

FEBRUARY 26

Dear Father,
Help us to love one another
with the love that comes from you.
For we know that everyone who loves is your child,
but whoever fails to love does not know you,
because you are love.
You revealed your love for us
by sending your only Son into the world
that we might have life through him.

Dear Father, if you loved us so much,
we too should love one another.
No one has ever seen you,
but as long as we love one another
you remain in us
and your love comes to its perfection in us.

Based on 1 John 4:7–14

FEBRUARY 27

Now unto him that is able to keep you from falling, and to present you faultless before the presence of his glory with exceeding joy, to the only wise God our Saviour, be glory and majesty, dominion and power, both now and ever. Amen.

Jude vv. 24–25

❄ FEBRUARY 28 ❄

How great and wonderful are all your works,
    Lord God Almighty;
upright and true are all your ways,
    King of nations.
Who does not revere and glorify your name, O Lord?
For you alone are holy,
    and all nations will come and adore you
    for the many acts of saving justice you have shown.

Revelation 15:3–4

MARCH

Praying with the Early Christians

❧ MARCH 1 ❧

You who called us to hope in your Name,
   which is first of all creation,
open the eyes of our heart
   that we may know you
who alone remains Highest among the highest
and Holiest among the holy.

Save those of us who are in affliction,
   have mercy on the lonely,
raise up those that are fallen,
   be manifested to those that are in need,
heal the sick,
   bring back those of your people that go astray.
Feed the hungry,
   redeem our captives,
lift up those that are weak,
   comfort the faint-hearted.

Clement of Rome, 1st century

❧ MARCH 2 ❧

May God the Father, and the eternal High Priest Jesus Christ, build us up in faith and truth and love, and grant us our portion among the saints with all those who believe on our Lord Jesus Christ. We pray for all saints, for kings and rulers, for the enemies of the cross of Christ, and for ourselves we pray that our fruit may abound and we be made perfect in Christ Jesus our Lord.

Polycarp, 69–155

❧ MARCH 3 ❧

O Lamb of God, who takest away the sin of the world, look upon us and have mercy upon us; thou who art thyself both victim and Priest, thyself

both Reward and Redeemer, keep safe from all evil those whom thou
hast redeemed, O Saviour of the world.

Irenaeus of Lyons, c. 130–200

❋ MARCH 4

We give you thanks, holy Father,
for your holy name,
which you planted in our hearts;
and for the knowledge, faith and immortality
which you sent us through Jesus Christ, your child.

Glory to you throughout the ages.

You created everything, sovereign Lord,
for the glory of your name.
You gave food and drink to men
for their enjoyment,
and as a cause for thanksgiving.
And to us you have given
spiriual food and spiritual drink,
bestowing on us the promise of eternal life.
Above all we thank you
for the power of your love.

Glory to you throughout the ages.

Deliver your Church, Lord, from all evil
and teach it to love you perfectly.
You have made it holy.
Build it up from the four winds
And gather it into the kingdom
for which you have destined it.

Power and glory to you throughout the ages.

The Didache, 1st or 2nd century

Lord Almighty,
the God of our fathers,
   we beseech you, hear us.

For the peace which is from above,
and for the salvation of our souls,
   let us beseech the Lord.

For the peace of the whole world,
and the unity of all the holy churches of God,
   let us beseech the Lord.

For the salvation
and help of all people who love Christ,
   we beseech you, hear us.

For our deliverance
from all tribulation, wrath,
danger, distress,
from captivity, bitter death,
and from our iniquities,
   we beseech you, hear us.

For the people here present,
and waiting for the rich and plenteous mercy
that is from you,
   we beseech you, be merciful and gracious.

Save your people, O Lord,
and bless your inheritance.
Visit your world in mercy and compassion,
   we beseech you, most merciful Lord.
Hear us praying to you,
   and have mercy upon us.

Liturgy of St James, 2nd century

❦ MARCH 6 ❦

We give you thanks,
yes, more than thanks, O Lord our God,
the Father of our Lord and God and Saviour Jesus Christ,
  for all your goodness
  at all times and in all places,
because you have shielded, rescued, helped,
and guided us all the days of our lives,
and brought us to this hour.

We pray and beseech you, merciful God,
to grant in your goodness
  that we may spend this holy day
  and all the time of our lives without sin,
  in fullness of joy, health, safety, holiness,
  and reverence of you.

But all envy, all fear, all temptation,
  all the influence of Satan,
  all the snares of the wicked,
O Lord, drive away from us,
and from your Holy Catholic and Apostolic Church.

Bestow upon us, O Lord, what is good and meet.
Whatever sin we commit in thought, word or deed,
in your goodness and mercy
be pleased to pardon.

Leave us not, O Lord, while we hope in you;
  nor lead us into temptation,
but deliver us from the evil one and from his works
through the grace, mercy and love
  of your Only-Begotten Son.

Through whom and with whom be glory and power to you,
in your most holy, good and life-giving Spirit,
now, henceforth, and for ever more.
Amen.

Liturgy of St Mark, 2nd century

❀ MARCH 7 ❀

May I be no man's enemy, and may I be the friend of that which
is eternal and abides.

May I never quarrel with those nearest me: and if I do, may I be
reconciled quickly.

May I love, seek, and attain only that which is good.

May I wish for all men's happiness and envy none.

May I never rejoice in the ill-fortune of one who has wronged me.

When I have done or said what is wrong, may I never wait for the
rebuke of others, but always rebuke myself until I make amends.

May I win no victory that harms either me or my opponent.

May I reconcile friends who are angry with one another.

May I, to the extent of my power, give all needful help to my friends
and all who are in want.

May I never fail a friend who is in danger.

When visiting those in grief may I be able by gentle and healing words
to soften their pain.

May I respect myself.

May I always keep tame that which rages within me.

May I accustom myself to be gentle, and never be angry with people
because of circumstances.

May I never discuss who is wicked and what wicked things he has done,
but know good men and follow in their footsteps.

Eusebius, 3rd century

❀ MARCH 8 ❀

O Lord our God, who hast chased the slumber from our eyes, and once
more assembled us to lift up our hands unto thee and to praise thy just
judgments, accept our prayers and supplications, and give us faith and
love. Bless our coming in and our going out, our thoughts, words, and
works, and let us begin this day with the praise of the unspeakable
sweetness of thy mercy. Hallowed be thy name. Thy kingdom come;
through Jesus Christ our Lord.

Greek Liturgy, 3rd century

🌸 MARCH 9 🌸

Be kind to your little children, Lord. Be a gentle teacher, patient with our weakness and stupidity. And give us the strength and discernment to do what you tell us, and so grow in your likeness.

May we all live in the peace that comes from you. May we journey towards your city, sailing through the waters of sin untouched by the waves, borne serenely along by the Holy Spirit. Night and day may we give you praise and thanks, because you have shown us that all things belong to you, and all blessings are gifts from you. To you, the essence of wisdom, the foundation of truth, be glory for evermore.

Clement of Alexandria, c. 150–215

🌸 MARCH 10 🌸

You are
  the ever-living One.
You are
  without beginning, like the Father,
  and co-eternal with the Spirit.
You are
  he who made all things out of nothing.
You are
  the Prince of the angels.
You are
  he at whom the depths tremble.
You are
  he who is covered with light as with a garment.
You are
  he who made us, and fashioned us of earth.
You are
  he who formed things invisible.

From your presence the whole earth flees away.

Hippolytus of Rome, c. 165–235

MARCH 11

Come quickly to help me,
 O Lord God of my salvation,
for the battle is great
 and the adversaries are powerful.
The enemy is hostile,
 the invisible foe fighting through visible forms.
Come quickly, therefore, to help us,
 and assist us through your holy Son,
 our Lord Jesus Christ,
through whom you have redeemed us all,
through whom be glory and power to you
 for ever and ever.
Amen.

Origen of Alexandria, c. 185–254

MARCH 12

Good God,
may we confess your name to the end.
May we emerge unsullied and glorious
from the traps and dark powers of this world.
As you have bound us together
in love and peace,
and as, together, we have persevered
through times of hardship,
may we also rejoice together
in your heavenly kingdom.

Cyprian of Carthage, c. 200–58

MARCH 13

O God of peace, good beyond all that is good, in whom is calmness and concord. Do thou make up the dissensions which divide us from one another, and bring us into unity of love in thee; through Jesus Christ our Lord.

Dionysius of Alexandria, c. 190–265

🌸 MARCH 14 🌸

Our eternal Saviour, King of gods,
you alone are almighty,
you are the Lord, the God of all beings,
and the God of our fathers.
You, the God of Abraham, Isaac and Jacob, are merciful,
compassionate, long-suffering and rich in mercy.
To you every heart is open,
and every secret thought is revealed.
The souls of the righteous cry out to you,
and the hope of the godly rests confidently in you.

You, Lord, are a Father to the righteous,
you hear the prayers of the upright,
and you know, too, the prayers that remain unuttered;
for your providence reaches even to the human heart,
your all-seeing gaze searches everyone's thoughts,
and from all around the world, like incense,
prayer and supplication rise up to you.

You have created the world to be a battlefield,
where our faith will be tried;
yet you have also opened to all the gate of mercy,
and have made clear to us
that the possession of riches is not everlasting;
that beauty will not last;
and that strength and power are likewise easily gone.

Only the fruit of true faith will last:
the only thing that will last and take us to heaven,
is the possession of a life of true faith.
That alone guarantees for us
the inheritance of the joy that is to come.

Apostolic Constitutions, 4th century

❦ MARCH 15 ❦

Lord our God, great, eternal, wonderful in glory, who keepest
covenant and promises for those that love thee with their whole
heart, who art the Life of all, the Help of those that flee unto thee,
the Hope of those who cry unto thee, cleanse us from our sins, secret
and open; and from every thought displeasing to thy goodness,
cleanse our bodies and souls, our hearts and consciences, that with a
pure heart, and a clean soul, with perfect love and calm hope, we may
venture confidently and fearlessly to pray unto thee, through Jesus
Christ our Lord.

Liturgy of St Basil, 4th century

❦ MARCH 16 ❦

O Lord, you have freed us from the fear of death. You have made the
end of our life here into the beginning of true life for us. You give rest to
our bodies for a time in sleep, and then you awaken them again with the
sound of the last trumpet. Our earthly body, formed by your hands, you
consign in trust to the earth, and then once more you reclaim it,
transfiguring with immortality and grace whatever in us is mortal or
deformed. You have opened for us the way to resurrection, and given to
those that fear you the sign of the holy cross as their emblem, to destroy
the enemy and to save our life.

Eternal God, on you have I depended from my mother's womb, you
have I loved with all the strength of my soul, to you have I dedicated my
flesh and my soul from my youth until now. Set by my side an angel of
light, to guide me to the place of repose, where are the waters of rest,
among the holy Fathers. You have broken the fiery sword and restored to
Paradise the thief who was crucified with you and implored your mercy:
remember me also in your kingdom, for I too have been crucified with
you. Let not the dread abyss separate me from your elect. Let not the
envious one bar the way before me. But forgive me and accept my soul
into your hands, spotless and undefiled, as incense in your sight.

Macrina, 4th century

✿ MARCH 17 ✿

Lord, we pray to you,
knowing you watch over us.
You not only created our souls and made our bodies,
you are the Saviour, Ruler and Guide of all people.
You love us so much
that you give us reconciliation and peace.

Be kind to us, Lord;
help and heal those who are ill,
cure their diseases;
and raise up those who are depressed.
We glorify your holy Name through Jesus Christ,
your only Son.
By him may power and glory be yours,
in the Holy Spirit,
now and age after age.
Amen.

Serapion of Thmuis, 4th century

✿ MARCH 18 ✿

You are God and we praise you; you are the Lord and we acclaim you;
You are the eternal Father; all creation worships you.
To you all angels, all the powers of heaven,
Cherubim and seraphim sing in endless praise,
Holy holy holy Lord, God of power and might;
Heaven and earth are full of your glory.
The glorious company of apostles praise you;
The noble fellowship of prophets praise you;
The white-robed army of martyrs praise you.
Throughout the whole world the holy church acclaims you,
Father of majesty unbounded;
Your true and only Son worthy of all worship,
And the Holy Spirit advocate and guide.

You Christ are the King of glory,
The eternal Son of the Father.
When you became man to set us free
You did not abhor the virgin's womb.
You overcame the sting of death
And opened the kingdom of heaven to all believers.
You are seated at God's right hand in glory;
We believe that you will come and be our judge.
Come then Lord and help your people,
Bought with the price of your own blood;
And bring us with your saints
To glory everlasting.

Te Deum, 4th century

🌼 MARCH 19 🌼

Although I am dust and ashes, Lord, I am tied to you by bonds of love.
Therefore I feel I can speak freely to you. Before I came to know you,
I was nothing. I did not know the meaning of life, and I had no
understanding of myself. I have no doubt that you had a purpose in
causing me to be born; yet you had no need of me, and on my own I was
of no use to you. But then you decided that I should hear the words of
your Son, Jesus Christ. And that as I heard his words, you enabled his
love to penetrate my heart. Now I am completely saturated in his love
and faith, and there is no remedy. Now, Lord, I cannot change my
attitude to my faith; I can only die for it.

Hilary of Poitiers, c. 310–67

🌼 MARCH 20 🌼

Lord Jesus Christ,
King of kings:
you have power over life and death,
you know even that which is not clear, but hard to understand,

what I think and feel is not hidden from you.
Therefore, cleanse me from my hidden sins,
for you have seen the wrong I have done.

As each day passes,
the end of my life becomes ever nearer,
and my sins increase in number.
You, Lord, my Creator, know how feeble I am,
and in my weakness, strengthen me;
when I suffer, uphold me,
and I will glorify you,
my Lord and God.

Ephraem of Syria, c. 306–73

🕮 MARCH 21 🕮

O God, enlarge within us the sense of fellowship with all living things,
our brothers the animals to whom thou gavest the earth as their home
in common with us.

We remember with shame that in the past we have exercised the high
dominion of man with ruthless cruelty so that the voice of the earth,
which should have gone up to thee in song, has been a groan of travail.
May we realize that they live not for us alone but for themselves and for
thee, and that they love the sweetness of life.

Basil the Great, c. 330–79

🕮 MARCH 22 🕮

You alone are unutterable,
from the time you created all things,
    that can be spoken of.
You alone are unknowable,
from the time you created all things
    that can be known.
All things cry out about you;

those which speak,
    and those which cannot speak.
All things honour you;
those which think,
    and those which cannot think.
For there is one longing, one groaning,
    that all things have for you...

All things pray to you
that comprehend your plan
    and offer you a silent hymn.
In you, the One, all things abide,
and all things endlessly run to you,
    who are the end of all.

Gregory of Nazianzus, 329–89

❀ MARCH 23 ❀

O eternal God, King of all creation, who hast brought me to this hour, forgive me the sins which I have committed this day in thought, word, and deed, and cleanse, O Lord, my humble soul from every stain of flesh and spirit.

Grant me, O Lord, to pass through the sleep of this night in peace, to rise from my lowly bed, to please thy holy name all the days of my life, and to vanquish the enemies both bodily and spiritual that contend against me.

Deliver me, O Lord, from the vain thoughts that stain me, and from evil desires. For thine is the kingdom and the power, and the glory, of the Father, and the Son, and the Holy Ghost, now and for ever and unto the ages of ages.

Macarius of Egypt, c. 300–90

❀ MARCH 24 ❀

O Lord, who hast mercy upon all, take away from me my sins, and mercifully kindle in me the fire of thy Holy Spirit. Take away from me the heart of stone, and give me a heart of flesh, a heart to love and adore thee, a heart to delight in thee, to follow and to enjoy thee, for Christ's sake.

Ambrose of Milan, c. 339–97

🏵 MARCH 25 🏵

O God of infinite mercy and boundless majesty,
whom no distance of place
nor length of time
can part from those for whom you care;
   be with your servants everywhere, who trust in you,
and through all the ways in which they are to go,
   be pleased to be their Guide and their Companion.

May no adversity harm them,
   no difficulty oppose them;
   may all things turn out happily and prosperously for them;
that by the help of your right hand,
whatever they have reasonably asked for,
   they may quickly receive a good response;
through Jesus Christ our Lord.

Gelasian Sacramentary, 5th century

🏵 MARCH 26 🏵

Worthy of praise from every mouth,
of confession from every tongue,
of worship from every creature,
is thy glorious name, O Father, Son, and Holy Ghost:
who didst create the world in thy grace
and by thy compassion didst save the world.
To thy majesty, O God, ten thousand times ten thousand
bow down and adore, singing and praising without ceasing and saying,

Holy, holy, holy, Lord God of hosts;
Heaven and earth are full of thy praises;
Hosanna in the highest.

Nestorian Liturgy, 5th century

🌑 MARCH 27 🌑

O God
be all my love,
all my hope,
all my striving;
let my thoughts and words flow from you,
my daily life be in you,
and every breath I take be for you.

John Cassian, 360–435 (adapted)

🌑 MARCH 28 🌑

Almighty God, unto whom all hearts are open, all desires known, and
from whom no secrets are hid; cleanse the thought of our hearts by the
inspiration of thy Holy Spirit, that we may perfectly love thee, and
worthily magnify thy holy Name, through Jesus Christ our Lord.

Gregorian Sacramentary, 6th century

🌑 MARCH 29 🌑

Grant calmness and control of thought to those who are facing
uncertainty and anxiety: let their heart stand fast, believing in the Lord.
Be thou all things to all men, knowing each one and his petition, each
house and its need, for the sake of Jesus Christ.

Russian Liturgy, 6th century

❦ MARCH 30 ❦

O thou whose reason guides the universe,
Maker of earth and heaven,
Who from eternity dost send forth time
And thyself motionless
Giv'st all things power to move.
No cause outside thyself prevailed on thee
To fashion floating matter to a world,
But an instinctive pattern in thy mind.
Utterly good, and with no taint of malice
Thou didst fashion all things in that heavenly mould.
Thou the supreme beauty in thy mind, didst shape
A perfect whole and made it then release
Its perfect parts: numbered the elements,
That cold might contain fire, and dryness water:
Lest fire too pure might vanish into air,
Or weight of water drag down flooded earth.
O Father, give the spirit power to climb
To the fountain of all light, and be purified.
Break through the mists of earth, the weight of the clod,
Shine forth in splendour, thou that art calm weather,
And quiet resting place for faithful souls.
To see thee is the end and the beginning,
Thou carriest us, and thou dost go before,
Thou art the journey, and the journey's end.

Boethius, c. 480–524

❦ MARCH 31 ❦

O Lord God, the life of mortals, the light of the faithful, the strength of
those who labour, the repose of the dead; grant us a tranquil night, free
from all disturbances; that after an interval of quiet sleep, we may, by
thy bounty, at the return of light, be endued with activity from the Holy
Spirit, and enabled in security to render thanks to thee, through Jesus
Christ our Lord.

Mozarabic Liturgy, 7th century

APRIL

Praying with
the Celts

🌸 APRIL 1 🌸

As the rain hides the stars, as the autumn mist hides the hills, as the clouds veil the blue of the sky, so the dark happenings of my lot hide the shining of thy face from me. Yet, if I may hold thy hand in the darkness, it is enough. Since I know that, though I may stumble in my going, thou dost not fall.

Anonymous

🌸 APRIL 2 🌸

Bless to me, O God,
 The earth beneath my foot,
Bless to me, O God,
 The path whereon I go;
Bless to me, O God,
 The thing of my desire;
  Thou Evermore of evermore,
 Bless Thou to me my rest.

Bless to me the thing
 Whereon is set my mind,
Bless to me the thing
 Whereon is set my love;
Bless to me the thing
 Whereon is set my hope,
  O Thou King of kings,
 Bless Thou to me mine eye!

Carmina Gadelica, Vol. III, page 181

🌸 APRIL 3 🌸

Be the eye of God between me and each eye,
Between me and each purpose God's purpose lie,
Be the hand of God between me and each hand,
Between me and each shield the shield of God stand,

God's desire between me and each desire be,
Be God's bridle between each bridle and me,
    And no man's mouth able to curse me I see.

Between me and each pain the pain of Christ show,
Between me and each love the love of Christ grow,
Between me and each dearness Christ's dearness stay,
Christ's kindness between me and each kindness aye,
Between me and each wish the wish of Christ found,
Between me and each will the will of Christ bound,
    And no venom can wound me, make me unsound.

Be the might of Christ between me and each might,
Be the right of Christ between me and each right,
Flow of the Spirit between me and each flow,
Between me and each lave the Spirit's lave go,
Between me and each bathe the Spirit's bathe clean,
    And to touch me no evil thing can be seen.

Poems of the Western Highlanders

🌸 APRIL 4 🌸

Be thou my Vision, O Lord of my heart,
Be all else but naught to me, save that thou art;
Be thou my best thought in the day and the night,
Both waking and sleeping, thy presence my light.

Be thou my Wisdom, be thou my true Word;
Be thou ever with me, and I with thee, Lord;
Be thou my great Father, and I thy true son;
Be thou in me dwelling, and I with thee one.

Be thou my Breastplate, my sword for the fight;
Be thou my whole armour, be thou my true might;
Be thou my soul's shelter, be thou my strong tower,
O raise thou me heavenward, great Power of my power.

Riches I heed not, nor man's empty praise,
Be thou mine inheritance now and always;

Be thou and thou only the first in my heart;
O Sovereign of heaven, my treasure thou art.

High King of heaven, thou heaven's bright Sun,
O grant me its joys, after victory is won;
Great Heart of my own heart, whatever befall,
Still be thou my Vision, O Ruler of all.

Anonymous

🌼 APRIL 5 🌼

Each day in justice let me speak,
Each day thy chastening marks, O God, display,
Each day in wisdom let me speak,
Each night at peace with thee, at peace each day;

Each day thy mercy's causes store,
Each day may I compose to thee a song,
Each day give heedance to thy law,
Each day string out, O God, thy praises strong;

Each day love let me give to thee,
Each night, O Jesu, grant I do the same,
Each day and night laud give to thee
Or dark or light, for goodness of thy Name,
Or dark or light,
Each day and night.

Poems of the Western Highlanders

🌼 APRIL 6 🌼

Give us, O God, the needs the body feels,
Give us, God, the need-things of the soul;
Give us, O God, the balm which body heals,
Give us, God, the soul-balm which makes whole.

Bliss give us, O God, of repentance-ease,
 Bliss give us, God, of forgiveness sought,
Away from us wash thou corruption's lees,
 From us wipe the blush of unclean thought.

O great God, thou who art upon the throne,
 Give to us the heart repentance true,
Forgiveness give us of the sin we own—
 The sin inborn and the sin we do.

Give us, O God, a yearning that is strong,
 And the crown of glory of the King;
Give us the safe home, God, for which we long
 In thy kingdom's lovely gates to sing.

May Michael, archangel warrior white,
 Keep down hostile demons of the fall;
May Jesus Christ MacDavid guide our flight
 And give lodging in his peace-bright hall.

Poems of the Western Highlanders

🌸 APRIL 7 🌸

God, give thy blest angels charge to surround
 Watching over this steading tonight,
A sacred, strong, steadfast band be they found
 To keep this soul-shrine from mischief-spite.

Safeguard thou, O God, this household tonight,
 Themselves, their means of life, their repute,
Free them from danger, from death, mischief-spite,
 From jealousy's and from hatred's fruit.

O grant thou to us, O God of our peace,
 Whate'er be our loss a thankful heart,
To obey thy laws here below nor cease,
 To enjoy thee when yon we depart.

Poems of the Western Highlanders

🕸 APRIL 8 🕸

God help my thoughts! they stray from me, setting off on the wildest journeys; when I am at prayer, they run off like naughty children, making trouble. When I read the Bible, they fly to a distant place, filled with seductions. My thoughts can cross an ocean with a single leap; they can fly from earth to heaven, and back again, in a single second. They come to me for a fleeting moment, and then away they flee. No chains, no locks can hold them back; no threats of punishment can restrain them, no hiss of a lash can frighten them. They slip from my grasp like tails of eels; they swoop hither and thither like swallows in flight.

Dear, chaste Christ, who can see into every heart, and read every mind, take hold of my thoughts. Bring my thoughts back to me, and clasp me to yourself.

Anonymous

🕸 APRIL 9 🕸

I am bending my knee
In the eye of the Father who created me,
In the eye of the Son who purchased me,
In the eye of the Spirit who cleansed me,
    In friendship and affection.
Through Thine own Anointed One, O God,
Bestow upon us fullness in our need,
        Love towards God,
        The affection of God,
        The smile of God,
        The wisdom of God,
        The grace of God,
        The fear of God,
        And the will of God
To do on the world of the Three,
As angels and saints
Do in heaven;
    Each shade and light,

Each day and night,
Each time in kindness,
Give Thou us thy Spirit.

Carmina Gadelica, Vol. I, page 3

🎕 APRIL 10 🎕

I am giving Thee worship with my whole life,
    I am giving Thee assent with my whole power,
I am giving Thee praise with my whole tongue,
    I am giving Thee honour with my whole utterance.

I am giving Thee reverence with my whole understanding,
    I am giving Thee offering with my whole thought,
I am giving Thee praise with my whole fervour,
    I am giving Thee humility in the blood of the Lamb.

I am giving Thee love with my whole devotion,
    I am giving Thee kneeling with my whole desire,
I am giving Thee love with my whole heart,
    I am giving Thee affection with my whole sense;
I am giving Thee my existence with my whole mind,
    I am giving Thee my soul, O God of all gods.

Carmina Gadelica, Vol. III, pages 41–45

🎕 APRIL 11 🎕

I believe, O God of all gods,
    That Thou art the eternal Father of life;
I believe, O God of all gods,
    That Thou art the eternal Father of love.

I believe, O God of all gods,
    That Thou art the eternal Father of the saints;
I believe, O God of all gods,
    That Thou art the eternal Father of each one.

I believe, O God of all gods,
    That Thou art the eternal Father of mankind;
 I believe, O God of all gods,
    That Thou art the eternal Father of the world.

I believe, O Lord and God of the peoples,
That Thou art the creator of the high heavens,
That Thou art the creator of the skies above,
That Thou art the creator of the oceans below.

I believe, O Lord and God of the peoples,
    That Thou art He Who created my soul and set its warp,
Who created my body from dust and from ashes,
    Who gave to my body breath, and to my soul its possession.

Father, bless to me my body,
Father, bless to me my soul,
Father, bless to me my life,
Father, bless to me my belief.

Carmina Gadelica, Vol. III, pages 41–45

🌸 APRIL 12 🌸

I bind unto myself today
    The power of God to hold and lead,
His eye to watch, his might to stay,
    His ear to hearken to my need,
The wisdom of my God to teach,
    His hand to guide, his shield to ward,
The Word of God to give me speech,
    His heavenly host to be my guard.

Christ be with me, Christ within me,
Christ behind me, Christ before me,
Christ beside me, Christ to win me,
Christ to comfort and restore me,

Christ beneath me, Christ above me,
Christ in quiet, Christ in danger,
Christ in hearts of all that love me,
Christ in mouth of friend and stranger.

Patrick, c. 390–460 (attributed)

🌼 APRIL 13 🌼

I will kindle my fire this morning
In presence of the holy angels of heaven,
In presence of Ariel of the loveliest form,
In presence of Uriel of the myriad charms,
Without malice, without jealousy, without envy,
Without fear, without terror of any one under the sun,
But the Holy Son of God to shield me.
 Without malice, without jealousy, without envy,
 Without fear, without terror of any one under the sun,
 But the Holy Son of God to shield me.

God, kindle Thou in my heart within
A flame of love to my neighbour,
To my foe, to my friend, to my kindred all,
To the brave, to the knave, to the thrall,
O Son of the loveliest Mary,
From the lowliest thing that liveth,
To the Name that is highest of all.
 O Son of the loveliest Mary,
 From the lowliest thing that liveth,
 To the Name that is highest of all.

Carmina Gadelica, Vol. I, page 231

Jesu MacMary, have mercy upon us;
Jesu MacMary, thy peace be upon us;
   Where we shall longest be,
   With us and for us be,
   Amen, eternally.

Jesu MacMary, at dawn-tide, the flowing,
Jesu MacMary, at ebb-tide, the going;
   When our first breath awakes,
   Life's day when darkness takes,
Merciful God of all, mercy bestowing,
   With us and for us be,
   Merciful Deity,
   Amen, eternally.

Condition and lot, to thee make them holy,
Condition and lot, to thee take them wholly,
   King of all kings that be,
   God of all things that be,
   Amen, eternally.

Our rights and our means, to thee make them holy,
Our rights and our means, to thee take them wholly,
   King of all kings that be,
   God of all things that be,
   Amen, eternally.

Our body and heart, to thee make them holy,
Our body and heart, to thee take them wholly,
   King of all kings that be,
   God of all things that be,
   Amen, eternally.

Each body and heart, the whole of each being,
Each day, each night also, thine overseeing,
   King of all kings that be,
   God of all things that be,
   Amen, eternally.

Poems of the Western Highlanders

❧ APRIL 15 ❧

May the Holy Ghost distilling,
　　Down from heaven forth to ground,
Grant me aid and goodness filling,
　　That my prayer be firmly bound,
The King of life's great throne around.

May the Holy Ghost with blessing
　　Wing the prayer I send as dove
In the fitting state and gracing
　　Of thy holy will above,
O Lord my God of life and love.

Be I in God's love, God's dearness,
　　Be I in God's will, God's sight,
Be I in God's choice, God's nearness,
　　Be I in God's charge, God's might,
And be I in God's keep aright.

As thine angels fair, untiring,
　　As thy saints, household entire,
They in heav'n above desiring,
　　So on earth may I desire,
With Holy Ghost aflame in fire.

Poems of the Western Highlanders

❧ APRIL 16 ❧

May the road rise up to meet you,
may the wind be always at your back,
may the sun shine upon your face,
the rains fall soft upon your fields
and, until we meet again,
may God hold you in the palm of his hand.

Anonymous

My dear King, my own King, without pride, without sin, you created the whole world, eternal, victorious King.

King above the elements, King above the sun, King beneath the ocean, King of the north and south, the east and west, against you no enemy can prevail.

King of the Mysteries, you existed before the elements, before the sun was set in the sky, before the waters covered the ocean floor; beautiful King, you are without beginning and without end.

King, you created the daylight, and made the darkness; you are not arrogant or boastful, and yet strong and firm.

King, you created the land out of shapeless mass, you carved the mountains and chiselled the valleys, and covered the earth with trees and grass.

King, you stretched out the sky above the earth, a perfect sphere like a perfect apple, and you decorated the sky with stars to shine at night.

King, you pierced the earth with springs from which pure water flows, to form streams and rivers across the land.

King, you ordained the eight winds, the four primary winds from north and south, east and west, and the four lesser winds that swirl hither and thither.

You gave each wind its own colour: the north wind is white, bringing snow in winter; the south wind is red, carrying warmth in summer; the west wind is blue, a cooling breeze across the sea; the east wind is yellow, scorching in summer and bitter in winter; and the lesser winds are green, orange, purple and black—the black wind that blows in the darkest nights.

King, you measured each object and each span within the universe: the heights of the mountains and the depths of the oceans; the distance from the sun to the moon, and from star to star.

You ordained the movements of every object: the sun to cross the sky each day, and the moon to rise each night; the clouds to carry rain from the sea, and the rivers to carry water back from the sea.

King, you divided the earth into three zones: the north cold and bitter; the south hot and dry; and the middle zone cool, wet and fertile.

And you created men and women to be your stewards of the earth, always praising you for your boundless love.

Oengus the Culdee, 9th century (attributed)

✦ APRIL 18 ✦

My prayer to thee, O God, pray I this day,
Voice I this day in thy mouth's voicing way,
As hold the men of heaven this day I hold,
Spend I this day as spends thine own household,
Under thy laws, O God, this day I go,
As saints in heaven pass pass I this day so.

Thou loving Christ who hangedst on the tree,
Each day, each night, thy compact mindeth me;
Lie down or rise unto thy cross I cede,
In life and death thou health and peace indeed,

Each day thy mercies' source let me recall,
Gentle, gen'rous bestowing on me all;
Each day in love to thee more full be I
For love to me that thou didst amplify.

From thee it came, each thing I have received,
From love it comes, each thing my hope conceived,
Thy bounty gives each thing that gives me zest,
Of thy disposing each thing I request.

God holy, loving Father, of the word
Everlasting, this living prayer be heard:
Understanding lighten, my will enfire,
Begin my doing and my love inspire,
My weakness strengthen, enfold my desire.

Cleanse heart, faith confirm, sanctify my soul,
Circle my body, and my mind keep whole;

As from my mouth my prayer upriseth clear,
May I feel in my heart that thou art here.

Poems of the Western Highlanders

🌸 APRIL 19 🌸

O God, all thanks be unto thee,
O God, all praise be unto thee,
O God, worship be unto thee,
For all that thou hast given me.

As thou didst give my body life
To earn for me my drink and food,
So grant to me eternal life
To show forth all thy glory good.

Through all my life grant to me grace,
Life grant me at the hour of death;
God with me at my leaving breath,
God with me in deep currents' race.

O God, in the breath's parting sigh,
O, with my soul in currents deep,
Sounding the fords within thy keep,
Crossing the deep floods, God be nigh.

Poems of the Western Highlanders

🌸 APRIL 20 🌸

O helper of workers,
ruler of all the good,
guard on the ramparts
and defender of the faithful,
who lift up the lowly
and crush the proud,

ruler of the faithful,
enemy of the impenitent,
judge of all judges,
who punish those who err,
pure life of the living,
light and Father of lights
shining with great light,
denying to none of the hopeful
your strength and help,
I beg that me, a little man
trembling and most wretched,
rowing through the infinite storm of this age,
Christ may draw after him to the lofty
most beautiful haven of life.

Columba, c. 521–97

🌸 APRIL 21 🌸

O Jesu, the one who art sinless quite,
Thou humble King of the meek and the poor,
Who wast brought low and crucified so sore
By sentence of the evil men of spite,
Do thou defend and shield me for this night
From traitor-ways and Judas-dark-steal flight.

My soul on thine own arm, O Christ, to lie,
Thou art the King of the City of Heaven,
Thou it was, Jesu, who my soul didst buy,
For by thee was my life-sacrifice given.

Do thou protect me because of my woe,
For the sake of thy passion, wounds, thy blood,
Take me in safety tonight as I go
Climbing up near to the City of God.

Poems of the Western Highlanders

❦ APRIL 22 ❦

O Lord God, destroy and root out whatever the adversary plants in me, that with my sins destroyed you may sow understanding and good work in my mouth and heart; so that in act and in truth I may serve only you and know how to fulfil the commandments of Christ and to seek yourself. Give me love, give me chastity, give me faith, give me all things which you know belong to the profit of my soul. O Lord, work good in me, and provide me with what you know that I need.

Columbanus, c. 543–615

❦ APRIL 23 ❦

O Son of God, do a miracle for me, and change my heart; thy having taken flesh to redeem me was more difficult than to transform my wickedness.

It is thou who, to help me, didst go to be scourged… thou, dear child of Mary, art the refined molten metal of our forge.

It is thou who makest the sun bright, together with the ice; it is thou who createdst the rivers and the salmon all along the river.

That the nut-tree should be flowering, O Christ, it is a rare craft; through thy skill too comes the kernel, thou fair ear of our wheat.

Though the children of Eve ill deserve the bird-flocks and the salmon, it was the Immortal One on the cross who made both salmon and birds.

It is he who makes the flower of the sloes grow through the surface of the blackthorn, and the nut-flower on other trees; beside this, what miracle is greater?

Tadhg Og O Huiginn, 15th century

❦ APRIL 24 ❦

O thou great God, thy light grant to me,
O thou great God, thy grace may I see,

O thou great God, thy felicity,
And in thy health's well cleanse me pure-white.

O God, lift from me mine anguish sore,
O God, lift from me what I abhor,
O God, lift from me vanity's store,
And lighten my soul in thy love's light.

As I shed off my clothing at night,
Grant that I shed off my conflict-plight,
As vapours lift off the hill-crests white,
Lift thou my soul from the mist of death.

O Jesu Christ, O MacMary One,
O Jesu Christ, O thou Paschal Son,
My body shield in thy shield-cloak spun,
My soul made white in thy white grace-breath.

Poems of the Western Highlanders

❦ APRIL 25 ❦

Peace between neighbours,
Peace between kindred,
Peace between lovers,
    In love of the King of life.

Peace between person and person,
Peace between wife and husband,
Peace between woman and children,
    The peace of Christ above all peace.

Bless, O Christ, my face,
    Let my face bless every thing;
Bless, O Christ, mine eye,
    Let mine eye bless all it sees.

Carmina Gadelica, Vol. III, page 267

🏵 APRIL 26 🏵

Peace of the running waves to you,
Deep peace of the flowing air to you,
Deep peace of the quiet earth to you,
Deep peace of the shining stars to you,
Deep peace of the shades of night to you,
Moon and stars always giving light to you,
Deep peace of Christ, the Son of Peace, to you.

Anonymous

🏵 APRIL 27 🏵

That thou wouldest give us perseverance in good works:
    we beseech thee to hear us...
That thou wouldest grant us that charity which the world cannot give:
    we beseech thee to hear us.

Christ is victor; Christ is king; Christ is lord of all.

Thou, O Christ, grant to us thy grace.
Thou, O Christ, give to us joy and peace.
Thou, O Christ, grant to us life and salvation.

Almighty and most bountiful God, we humbly implore thy Majesty,
that... thou wouldest grant to us pardon and forgiveness of all our sins,
the increase of thy heavenly grace, and thine effectual help against all
snares of our enemies visible and invisible, inasmuch as our hearts also
are given up wholly to thy commandments, so that, at the last, after this
mortal life is ended, we may see the face and glory of thy saints in the
kingdom of God, and be counted worthy to rejoice with them in our
most glorious lord Jesus Christ our redeemer; to whom be glory and
honour and power and dominion, with the Father and the Holy Ghost,
throughout all ages. Amen.

Litany of Dunkeld, 9th century

APRIL 28

Thou angel of God who hast charge of me
From the dear Father of mercifulness,
The shepherding kind of the fold of the saints
To make round about me this night;

Drive from me every temptation and danger,
Surround me on the sea of unrighteousness,
And in the narrows, crooks, and straits,
Keep thou my coracle, keep it always.

Be thou a bright flame before me,
Be thou a guiding star above me,
Be thou a smooth path below me,
And be a kindly shepherd behind me,
To-day, to-night, and for ever.

I am tired and I a stranger,
Lead thou me to the land of angels;
For me it is time to go home
To the court of Christ, to the peace of heaven.

Carmina Gadelica, Vol. I, page 49

APRIL 29

The Father who created me
With eye benign beholdeth me;
The Son who dearly purchased me
With eye divine enfoldeth me;
The Spirit who so altered me
With eye refining holdeth me;
In friendliness and love the Three
Behold me when I bend the knee.

O God, through thine Anointed One,
The fullness of our needs be done—
Grant us towards God the love ordained,
Grant us towards man the love unfeigned;
Grant us the smile of God's good face,
Grant us God's wisdom and God's grace;
Grant us to fear and reverence still,
Grant in the world to do thy will
As done in heaven by saintly hands
And myriad of angelic bands;
Each day and night, each dawn and fall,
Grant us in kindness, Lord of all,
Thy nature's tincture at our call.

Poems of the Western Highlanders

🌸 APRIL 30 🌸

'Tis God's will I would do,
My own will I would rein;
Would give to God his due,
From my own due refrain;
God's path I would pursue,
My own path would disdain;

For Christ's death would I care,
My own death duly weighed;
Christ's pain my silent prayer,
My God-love warmer made;
'Tis Christ's cross I would bear,
My own cross off me laid;

Repentance I would make,
Repentance early choose;
Rein for my tongue would take,
Rein for my thoughts would use;

God's judgment would I mind,
My own judgment close-scanned;
Christ's freedom seizing bind,
My own freedom in hand;
Christ's love close-scanned would find,
My own love understand.

Poems of the Western Highlanders

MAY

Praying with Medieval Christians

❧ MAY 1 ❧

May the Lord be my friend,
Who once on earth endured on the gallows-tree
Suffered here for the sins of men.
He has redeemed us, he has given us life
And a home in Heaven. Hope was renewed
With bliss and blessing for those who had been through burning.
The Son was successful in that expedition,
Mighty in victory, when with a mass,
A great crowd of souls, came to God's kingdom
The Almighty Ruler, to joy among the angels
And all the saints, who in heaven already
Lived in glory, then the Lord
Almighty God, came home to his own land.

The Dream of the Rood, 8th century

❧ MAY 2 ❧

Almighty and merciful God, the fountain of all goodness, who knowest
the thoughts of our hearts, we confess unto thee that we have sinned
against thee, and done evil in thy sight. Wash us, we beseech thee, from
the stains of our past sins, and give us grace and power to put away all
hurtful things; so that, being delivered from the bondage of sin, we may
bring forth worthy fruits of repentance.

O eternal light, shine into our hearts. O eternal goodness, deliver us
from evil. O eternal power, be thou our support. Eternal wisdom, scatter
the darkness of our ignorance. Eternal pity, have mercy upon us. Grant
unto us that with all our hearts, and minds, and strength, we may
evermore seek thy face; and finally bring us, in thine infinite mercy, to
thy holy presence. So strengthen our weakness that, following in the
footsteps of thy blessed Son, we may obtain thy mercy, and enter into
thy promised joy.

Meuin, 8th century

❦ MAY 3 ❦

O God the Father, origin of divinity, good beyond all that is good, fair beyond all that is fair, in whom is calmness, peace, and concord; do thou make up the dissensions which divide us from each other, and bring us back into a unity of love, which may bear some likeness to thy divine nature. And as thou art above all things, make us one by the unanimity of a good mind, that through the embrace of charity and the bonds of affection, we may be spiritually one, as well in ourselves as in each other; through that peace of thine which maketh all things peaceful, and through the grace, mercy, and tenderness of thy Son, Jesus Christ.

Liturgy of St Dionysius, 9th century

❦ MAY 4 ❦

O King of glory and Lord of valours, who hast said, 'Be of good cheer, I have overcome the world': be thou victorious in us thy servants, for without thee we can do nothing. Grant thy compassion to go before us, thy compassion to come behind us: before us in our undertakings, behind us in our ending. And what more shall we say but that thy will be done; for thy will is our salvation, our glory, and our joy.

Alcuin, 735–804

❦ MAY 5 ❦

O thou who art the everlasting Essence of things beyond space and time and yet within them; thou who transcendest yet pervadest all things, manifest thyself unto us, feeling after thee, seeking thee in the shades of ignorance. Stretch forth thy hand to help us, who cannot without thee come to thee; and reveal thyself unto us, who seek nothing beside thee; through Jesus Christ our Lord.

Johannes Scotus Erigena, 810–90

❦ MAY 6 ❦

Lord God Almighty, Shaper and Ruler of all creatures, we pray thee for thy great mercy, that thou guide us better than we have done, towards thee. And guide us to thy will, to the need of our soul, better than we can ourselves. And steadfast our mind towards thy will and to our soul's need. And strengthen us against the temptations of the devil, and put far from us all lust, and every unrighteousness, and shield us against our foes, seen and unseen. And teach us to do thy will, that we may inwardly love thee before all things, with a pure mind. For thou art our Maker and our Redeemer, our Help, our Comfort, our Trust, our Hope; praise and glory be to thee now, ever and ever, world without end.

King Alfred, 849–901

❦ MAY 7 ❦

O Lord Jesus Christ, who crossed from this world to the Father, and loved those who were in the world, make my mind cross from earthly to heavenly things; make it despise all that is falling away and desire only heavenly things, and make me long to burn with the fire of your love. And you, O God, who condescended to wash with sacred hands the feet of your holy apostles, purify my heart by pouring upon it the light of the Holy Spirit, that in all things and above all things I may be able to love you, our Lord Jesus Christ. Amen.

From an Anglo-Saxon Prayer Book, ?10th century

❦ MAY 8 ❦

There was a time when I did not exist,
And thou hast created me;
I did not beseech thee for a wish,
And thou hast fulfilled it;
I had not come into the light,
And thou hast seen me;
I had not yet appeared,

And thou hast taken pity on me;
I had not invoked thee,
And thou hast taken care of me;
I did not raise my hand,
And thou hast looked at me;
I had not entreated thee,
And thou hast heard me;
I had not groaned,
And thou hast lent an ear;
With prescient eyes thou sawest
The crimes of my guilty self,
And yet thou hast fashioned me.
And now, I who have been created by thee,
And saved by thee,
And have been tended with such care,
Let me not wholly perish by the blow of sin
That is but the slanderer's invention;
Let not the fog of my stubbornness
Triumph over the light of thy forgiveness;
Nor the hardness of my heart
Over thy forbearing goodness;
Nor my material weakness
Over thine unconquerable grandeur.

Gregory of Narek, 951–1001

🌼 MAY 9 🌼

Lord Jesus Christ, Son of God, have mercy on me, a sinner.

'The Jesus Prayer', ?11th century

🌼 MAY 10 🌼

O thou who hast willed to be called Love, give me love, that I may love
thee more than I love myself, and care not at all what I do with myself,
so long as I am doing what is pleasing in thy sight. Grant me, O Father,

though I dare not always call myself thy child, at least to be thy faithful little servant and the sheep of thy pasture. Speak to thy servant's heart sometimes so that thy consolations may give joy to my soul. And teach me to speak to thee often in prayer. Take to thyself all my poverty and need, O Lord, my God and my Father. Have pity on my weakness, O my strength; and may it be to thy great glory that my feebleness continues to serve thee.

William of Saint Thierry, 1085–1148

🏵 MAY 11 🏵

Move our hearts with the calm, smooth flow of your grace. Let the river of your love run through our souls. May my soul be carried by the current of your love, towards the wide, infinite ocean of heaven.

Stretch out my heart with your strength, as you stretch out the sky above the earth. Smooth out any wrinkles of hatred or resentment, Enlarge my soul that it may know more fully your truth.

Gilbert of Hoyland, 12th century

🏵 MAY 12 🏵

O consuming Fire, Spirit of Love,
descend within me
and reproduce in me, as it were,
an incarnation of the Word,
that I may be to him
another humanity
wherein he renews his mystery.

Elizabeth of the Trinity, 12th century

❦ MAY 13 ❦

Lord, how much juice you can squeeze from a single grape.
How much water you can draw from a single well.
How great a fire you can kindle from a tiny spark.
How great a tree you can grow from a tiny seed.
My soul is so dry that by itself it cannot pray;
Yet you can squeeze from it the juice of a thousand prayers.
My soul is so parched that by itself it cannot love;
Yet you can draw from it boundless love for you and for my neighbour.
My soul is so cold that by itself it has no joy;
Yet you can light the fire of heavenly joy within me.
My soul is so feeble that by itself it has no faith;
Yet by your power my faith grows to a great height.
Thank you for prayer, for love, for joy, for faith;
Let me always be prayerful, loving, joyful, faithful.

Guigo the Carthusian, 12th century

❦ MAY 14 ❦

As the beautiful, dew-covered rose
   rises from amongst the thorns,
so may my heart be so full of love for you, my God,
   that I may rise above the storms and evils that assail me,
and stand fast in truth and freedom of spirit.

Hadewijch of Brabant, 13th century (adapted)

❦ MAY 15 ❦

God be in my head,
   And in my understanding;
God be in my eyes,
   And in my looking;
God be in my mouth,

And in my speaking;
God be in my heart,
And in my thinking;
God be at my end,
And at my departing.

Old Sarum primer, ?13th century

May 16

Now, our Lord Jesus Christ
give us grace, so to honour God,
and to love our fellow Christians,
and ourselves to be lowly of heart,
that we may for our honouring be honoured,
for our love be loved,
and for our meekness be lifted up
into the high bliss of heaven,
that Jesus bought for us
with his blood and most precious Passion.

Edmund Rich, 1170–1240

May 17

O Lord Jesus Christ, make me worthy to understand the profound mystery of your holy incarnation, which you have worked for our sake and for our salvation. Truly there is nothing so great and wonderful as this, that you, my God, who are the creator of all things, should become a creature, so that we should become like God. You have humbled yourself and made yourself small that we might be made mighty. You have taken the form of a servant, so that you might confer upon us a royal and divine beauty.

Angela of Foligno, 1248–1309

🕮 MAY 18 🕮

As a needle turns to the north when it is touched by the magnet, so it is
fitting, O Lord, that I, your servant, should turn to love and praise and
serve you; seeing that out of love to me you were willing to endure such
grievous pangs and sufferings.

Raymond Lull, 1235–1315

🕮 MAY 19 🕮

My God, I love thee above all else and thee I desire as my last end.
Always and in all things, with my whole heart, and strength I seek thee.
If thou give not thyself to me, thou givest nothing; if I find thee not, I
find nothing. Grant to me, therefore, most loving God, that I may ever
love thee for thyself above all things, and seek thee in all things in this
life present, so that at last I may find thee and keep thee for ever in the
world to come.

Thomas Bradwardine, c. 1290–1349

🕮 MAY 20 🕮

Jesus, receive my heart,
and bring me to thy love.
All my desire thou art.
Kindle fire within me,
that I may win to thy love,
and see thy face in bliss
which shall never cease,
in heaven with never an ending.

Richard Rolle, 1295–1349

❀ MAY 21 ❀

My soul hath desired thee all night, O eternal wisdom! and in the early morning I turn to thee from the depths of my heart. May thy holy presence remove all dangers from my soul and body. May thy many graces fill the inmost recesses of my heart, and inflame it with thy divine love.

O most sweet Jesus! turn thy face towards me, for this morning with all the power of my soul I fly to thee... May all that is beautiful and amiable in creatures praise thee for me, and may all creation bless thy holy name, our consoling protection in time and in eternity.

Henry Suso, c. 1295–1366

❀ MAY 22 ❀

Soul of Christ, sanctify me;
Body of Christ, save me;
Blood of Christ, flow in my veins;
Water from the side of Christ, wash me;
Passion of Christ, comfort me;

Good Jesu, hear me;
Within your wounds, hide me;
Never let me be separated from you;
From the deadly enemy, defend me;
In the hour of my death, call me,
And ask me to come to you,
That with the saints I may sing your praise
For ever and ever.

The 'Anima Christi', 14th century

❀ MAY 23 ❀

You are Wisdom, uncreated and eternal,
    the supreme first cause, above all being,
    sovereign Godhead, sovereign goodness,
    watching unseen the God-inspired wisdom of Christian people.

Raise us, we pray, that we may totally respond
    to the supreme, unknown, ultimate, and splendid height
    of your words, mysterious and inspired.
There all God's secret matters lie covered and hidden
    under darkness both profound and brilliant, silent and wise.
You make what is ultimate and beyond brightness
    secretly to shine in all that is most dark.
In your way, ever unseen and intangible,
    you fill to the full with most beautiful splendour
    those souls who close their eyes that they may see.
And I, please, with love that goes on beyond mind
    to all that is beyond mind,
    seek to gain such for myself through this prayer.

The Cloud of Unknowing, 14th century

❦ MAY 24 ❦

Lord, thou art in me and shalt never be lost out of me, but I am not
near thee till I have found thee. Nowhere need I run to seek thee, but
within me where already thou art. Thou art the treasure hidden within
me: draw me therefore to thee that I may find thee and serve and
possess thee for ever.

Walter Hilton, 14th century (adapted)

❦ MAY 25 ❦

Lord, thou knowest what I want,
if it be thy will that I have it,
and if it be not thy will,
good Lord, do not be displeased,
for I want nothing which you do not want.

Julian of Norwich, 1342–c. 1416

❧ MAY 26 ❧

Come down, O Love divine,
  Seek thou this soul of mine,
And visit it with thine own ardour glowing;
  O Comforter, draw near,
  Within my heart appear,
And kindle it, thy holy flame bestowing.

  O let it freely burn,
  Till earthly passions turn
To dust and ashes, in its heat consuming;
  And let thy glorious light
  Shine ever on my sight,
And clothe me round, the while my path illluming.

  Let holy charity
  Mine outward vesture be,
And lowliness become mine inner clothing;
  True lowliness of heart,
  Which takes the humbler part,
And o'er its own shortcomings weeps with loathing.

  And so the yearning strong,
  With which the soul will long,
Shall far outpass the power of human telling;
  For none can guess its grace,
  Till he become the place
Wherein the Holy Spirit makes his dwelling.

Bianco da Siena, 15th century

❧ MAY 27 ❧

Grant us, O Lord, to know that which is worth knowing, to love that
which is worth loving, to praise that which can bear with praise, to hate
what in thy sight is unworthy, to prize what to thee is precious, and,
above all, to search out and to do what is well-pleasing unto thee;
through Jesus Christ our Lord.

Thomas à Kempis, c. 1380–1471

❧ MAY 28 ❧

Lord, I pray not for tranquillity, nor that my tribulations may cease;
I pray for your spirit and your love, that thou grant us strength and
grace to overcome adversity; through Jesus Christ. Amen.

Girolamo Savonarola, 1452–98

❧ MAY 29 ❧

O most merciful Father, who dost put away the sins of those who truly
repent, we come before thy throne in the name of Jesus Christ, that for
his sake alone thou wilt have compassion upon us, and let not our sins
be a cloud between thee and us.

John Colet, 1467–1519

❧ MAY 30 ❧

Spirit of God, with your holy breath
you cleanse the hearts and minds of your people;
you comfort them when they are in sorrow;
you lead them when they wander from the way,
you kindle them when they are cold,
you knit them together when they are at variance,
and you enrich them with many and various gifts.
We beseech you daily to increase
those gifts which you have entrusted to us;
that with your light before us and within us
we may pass through this world
without stumbling and without straying.

Erasmus, 1466–1536

❦ MAY 31 ❦

O Lord, the author and persuader of peace, love and goodwill, soften our hard and steely hearts, warm our icy and frozen hearts, that we may wish one another well, and may be the true disciples of Jesus Christ. And give us grace even now to begin to display that heavenly life in which there is no disagreement or hatred, but peace and love on all hands, one towards another.

Ludovicus Vives, 1492–1540

JUNE

Praying with the Saints and Mystics

🌣 JUNE 1 🌣

I am not worthy, Master and Lord, that you should come beneath the roof of my soul; yet since in your love towards all, you wish to dwell in me, in boldness I come. You command; open the gates, which you alone have made. And you will come in, and enlighten my darkened reasoning. I believe that you will do this; for you did not send away the harlot who came to you with tears, nor cast out the repenting tax-collector, nor reject the thief who acknowledged your kingdom. But you counted all of these as members of your band of friends. You are blessed for evermore.

John Chrysostom, c. 347–407

🌣 JUNE 2 🌣

O thou good omnipotent,
who so carest for every one of us,
as if thou caredst for him alone;
and so for all,
as if all were but one!
Blessed is the man who loveth thee,
and his friend in thee, and his enemy for thee;
For he only loses none dear to him,
to whom all are dear in him who cannot be lost.
And who is that but our God,
the God that made heaven and earth, and filleth them,
even by filling them and creating them.
And thy law is truth,
and truth is thyself.
I behold how some things pass away
that others may replace them,
but thou dost never depart, O God,
my Father supremely good,
Beauty of all things beautiful.
To thee will I entrust
whatsoever I have received from thee,

so shall I lose nothing.
Thou madest me for thyself
and my heart is restless until it repose in thee.

Augustine, 354–430

🏵 JUNE 3 🏵

Lord Jesus, think on me,
And purge away my sin;
From earthborn passions set me free,
And make me pure within.

Lord Jesus, think on me,
With care and woe oppressed;
Let me thy loving servant be,
And taste thy promised rest.

Lord Jesus, think on me,
Nor let me go astray;
Through darkness and perplexity
Point thou the heavenly way.

Lord Jesus, think on me,
That when the flood is past,
I may the eternal brightness see,
And share thy joy at last.

Synesius, 375–430

🏵 JUNE 4 🏵

O gracious and holy Father
Give us wisdom to perceive thee,
intelligence to understand thee,
diligence to seek thee,
patience to wait for thee,
eyes to behold thee,

a heart to meditate upon thee,
and a life to proclaim thee;
through the power of the spirit
of Jesus Christ our Lord.

Benedict, 480–c. 550

🕮 JUNE 5 🕮

Lo, fainter now lie spread the shades of night,
    and upward spread the trembling gleams of morn,
suppliant we bend before the Lord of Light,
    and pray at early dawn,
that this sweet charity may all our sin
    forgive, and make our miseries to cease;
may grant us health, grant us the gift divine
    of everlasting peace.
Father Supreme, this grace on us confer;
    and thou, O Son by an eternal birth!
with thee, coequal Spirit, comforter!
    whose glory fills the earth.

Pope Gregory I, c. 540–604

🕮 JUNE 6 🕮

O God that art the only hope of the world,
The only refuge for unhappy men,
Abiding in the faithfulness of heaven,
Give me strong succour in this testing place.
O King, protect thy man from utter ruin
Lest the weak faith surrender to the tyrant,
Facing innumerable blows alone.
Remember I am dust, and wind, and shadow,
And life as fleeting as the flower of grass.

But may the eternal mercy which hath shone
From time of old
Rescue thy servant from the jaws of the lion.
Thou who didst come from on high in the cloak of flesh,
Strike down the dragon with that two-edged sword,
Whereby our mortal flesh can war with the winds
And beat down strongholds, with our Captain God.

Bede, 675–735

🌼 JUNE 7 🌼

Come, true light.
Come, life eternal.
Come, hidden mystery.
Come, treasure without name.
Come, reality beyond all words.
Come, person beyond all understanding.
Come, rejoicing without end.
Come, light that knows no evening.
Come, unfailing expectation of the saved.
Come, raising of the fallen.
Come, resurrection of the dead.
Come, all-powerful, for unceasingly you create, refashion and
    change all things by your will alone.
Come, invisible whom none may touch and handle.
Come, for you continue always unmoved, yet at every instant you
    are wholly in movement; you draw near to us who lie in hell, yet
    you remain higher than the heavens.
Come, for your name fills our hearts with longing and is ever on our lips;
    yet who you are and what your nature is, we cannot say or know.
Come, Alone to the alone.
Come, for you are yourself the desire that is within me.
Come, the consolation of my humble soul.
Ccome, my joy, my endless delight.

Symeon the New Theologian, 949–1022

❧ JUNE 8 ❧

O Lord my God,
  teach my heart where and how to seek you,
  where and how to find you.
  Lord, if you are not here but absent,
    where shall I seek you?
  But you are everywhere, so you must be here,
  why then do I not seek you?...
Lord, I am not trying to make my way to your heights,
for my understanding is in no way equal to that,
but I do desire to understand a little of your truth
  which my heart already believes and loves.
I do not seek to understand so that I may believe,
  but I believe so that I may understand;
    and what is more,
I believe that unless I do believe I shall not understand.

Anselm, 1033–1109

❧ JUNE 9 ❧

Let your goodness, Lord, appear to us, that we, made in your image,
conform ourselves to it. In our own strength we cannot imitate your
majesty, power and wonder; nor is it fitting for us to try. But your mercy
reaches from the heavens, through the clouds, to the earth below. You
have come to us as a small child, but you have brought us the greatest of
all gifts, the gift of eternal love. Caress us with your tiny hands, embrace
us with your tiny arms, and pierce our hearts with your soft, sweet cries.

Bernard of Clairvaux, 1090–1153

❧ JUNE 10 ❧

Thou knowest my heart, Lord,
that whatsoever thou hast given to thy servant,

I desire to spend wholly on your people
    and to consume it all in their service.
Grant unto me then, O Lord my God,
that thine eyes may be opened upon them day and night.
Tenderly spread thy care to protect them.
Stretch forth thy holy right hand to bless them.
Pour into their hearts thy Holy Spirit
who may abide with them while they pray,
to refresh them with devotion and penitence,
to stimulate them with hope,
to make them humble with fear,
and to inflame them with charity.
May he, the kind Consoler,
succour them in temptation
and strengthen them in all the tribulations of this life.

Aelred of Rievaulx, 1109–67

JUNE 11

O eternal God,
Now let it please you
To burn in that love
So that we become those limbs
Which you made in that same love
When you gave birth to your Son
In the first dawn
Before all creatures,
And look on this need
Which falls upon us.
Take it from us
For the sake of your Son
And lead us into the bliss of salvation.

Hildegard of Bingen, 1098–1179

❧ JUNE 12 ❧

Lord, make us to walk in your way:
'Where there is love and wisdom, there is neither fear nor ignorance;
where there is patience and humility, there is neither anger nor
    annoyance;
where there is poverty and joy, there is neither greed nor avarice;
where there is peace and contemplation, there is neither care nor
    restlessness;
where there is the fear of God to guard the dwelling, there no enemy
    can enter;
where there is mercy and prudence, there is neither excess nor harshness';
this we know through your Son, Jesus Christ our Lord.

Francis of Assisi, 1182–1226

❧ JUNE 13 ❧

Lord, since you exist, we exist. Since you are beautiful, we are beautiful.
Since you are good, we are good. By our existence we honour you.
By our beauty we glorify you. By our goodness we love you.

    Lord, through your power all things were made. Through your
wisdom all things are governed. Through your grace all things are
sustained. Give us power to serve you, wisdom to discern your laws, and
grace to obey those at all times.

Edmund of Abingdon, c. 1180–1240

❧ JUNE 14 ❧

I pray you, O most gentle Jesus, having redeemed me by baptism from
original sin, so now by your precious blood, which is offered and
received throughout the world, deliver me from all evils, past, present
and to come. By your most cruel death give me lively faith, a firm hope
and perfect charity, so that I may love you with all my heart and all my

soul and all my strength. Make me firm and steadfast in good works
and grant me perseverance in your service so that I may be able to
please you always.

Clare of Assisi, 1194–1253

JUNE 15

Thanks be to thee,
O Lord Christ,
for all the benefits which thou hast given us;
for all the pains and insults which thou hast borne for us.

O most merciful redeemer,
friend
and brother,
may we know thee more clearly,
love thee more dearly,
and follow thee more nearly;
for thine own sake.

Richard of Chichester, 1197–1253

JUNE 16

To thee, then O Jesus, do I turn my true and last end. Thou art the river
of life which alone can satisfy my thirst. Without thee all else is barren
and void. Without all else thou alone art enough for me. Thou art the
Redeemer of those that are lost; the sweet Consoler of the sorrowful; the
crown of glory for the victors; the recompense of the blessed. One day I
hope to receive of thy fullness, and to sing the song of praise in my true
home. Give me only on earth some few drops of consolation, and I will
patiently wait thy coming that I may enter into the joy of my Lord.

Bonaventure, 1221–74

❦ JUNE 17 ❦

O Creator past all telling,
you have so beautifully set out all parts of the universe;
you are the true fount of wisdom
and the noble origin of all things.
Be pleased to shed on the darkness of my mind
the beam and warmth of your light
to dispel my ignorance and sin.
Instruct my speech and touch my lips with graciousness;
make me keen to understand, quick to learn,
and able to remember;
and keep me finely tuned
to interpret your word,
for you are God for ever and ever.

Thomas Aquinas, 1255–74

❦ JUNE 18 ❦

O sweet and loving God,
When I stay asleep too long,
Oblivious to all your many blessings,
Then, please, wake me up,
And sing to me your joyful song.
It is a song without noise or notes.
It is a song of love beyond words,
Of faith beyond the power of human telling.
I can hear it in my soul,
When you awaken me to your presence.

Mechthild of Magdeburg, c. 1210–80

❦ JUNE 19 ❦

Lord, in union with your love, unite my work with your great work,
and perfect it. As a drop of water, poured into a river, is taken up into

the activity of the river, so may my labour become part of your work. Thus may those among whom I live and work be drawn into your love.

Gertrude the Great, 1256–c. 1302

🌸 JUNE 20 🌸

Dear Lord, it seems that you are so madly in love with your creatures that you could not live without us. So you created us; and then, when we turned away from you, you redeemed us. Yet you are God, and so have no need of us. Your greatness is made no greater by our creation; your power is made no stronger by our redemption. You have no duty to care for us, no debt to repay us. It is love, and love alone, which moves you.

Catherine of Siena, 1347–80

🌸 JUNE 21 🌸

Lord, I make you a present of myself. I do not know what to do with myself. So let me make this exchange: I will place myself entirely in your hands, if you will cover my ugliness with your beauty, and tame my unruliness with your love. Put out the flames of false passion in my heart, since these flames destroy all that is true within me. Make me always busy in your service.

Lord, I want no special signs from you, nor am I looking for intense emotions in response to your love. I would rather be free of all emotion, than to run the danger of falling victim once again to false passion. Let my love for you be naked, without any emotional clothing.

Catherine of Genoa, 1447–1510

🌸 JUNE 22 🌸

Glorious God, give me grace to amend my life, and to have an eye to my end without begrudging death, which to those who die in you, good Lord, is the gate of a wealthy life.

And give me, good Lord, a humble, lowly, quiet, peaceable, patient, charitable, kind, tender and pitiful mind, in all my works and all my words and all my thoughts, to have a taste of your holy, blessed Spirit.

Give me, good Lord, a full faith, a firm hope, and a fervent charity, a love of you incomparably above the love of myself.

Give me, good Lord, a longing to be with you, not to avoid the calamities of this world, nor so much to attain the joys of heaven, as simply for love of you.

And give me, good Lord, your love and favour, which my love of you, however great it might be, could not deserve were it not for your great goodness.

These things, good Lord, that I pray for, give me your grace to labour for.

Thomas More, 1478–1535

🕮 JUNE 23 🕮

My God, I love thee—not because
I hope for heaven thereby,
Not yet because who love thee not
Are lost eternally.

Thou, O my Jesus, thou didst me
Upon the cross embrace;
For me didst bear the nails and spear,
And manifold disgrace;

And griefs and torments numberless,
And sweat of agony,
Yea, death itself—and all for one
Who was thine enemy.

Then why, O blessed Jesus Christ,
Should I not love thee well?
Not for the sake of winning heaven,
Or of escaping hell;

Not with the hope of gaining aught;
Not seeking a reward;
But as thyself hast loved me,
O ever-loving Lord.

E'en so I love thee, and will love,
And in thy praise will sing;
Solely because thou art my God
And my eternal King.

Francis Xavier, 1506–52 (attributed)

🏵 JUNE 24 🏵

Dearest Lord, teach me to be generous;
Teach me to serve thee as thou deservest;
To give and not to count the cost,
To fight and not to heed the wounds,
To toil and not to seek for rest,
To labour and not to seek reward,
Save that of knowing that I do thy will.

Ignatius Loyola, 1491–1556

🏵 JUNE 25 🏵

Govern all by thy wisdom, O Lord, so that my soul may always be
serving thee as thou dost will, and not as I may choose. Do not punish
me, I beseech thee, by granting that which I wish or ask, if it offends thy
love, which would always live in me. Let me die to myself that so I may
serve thee; let me live to thee, who in thyself art the true life.

Teresa of Avila, 1515–82

🏵 JUNE 26 🏵

O blessed Jesus, give me stillness of soul in thee.
Let thy mighty calmness reign in me;
Rule me, O King of gentleness, King of peace.
Give me control, great power of self-control,
Control over my words, thoughts and actions.
From all irritability, want of meekness, want of gentleness,
    dear Lord, deliver me.
By thine own deep patience, give me patience.
Make me in this and all things more and more like thee.

John of the Cross, 1542–91

🏵 JUNE 27 🏵

Come, O Christ my Light, and illumine my darkness.
Come, my Life, and revive me from death.
Come, my Physician, and heal my wounds.
Come, Flame of divine love, and burn up the thorns of my sins,
kindling my heart with the flame of your love.
For you alone are my King and my Lord.

Dimitrii of Rostov, 17th century

🏵 JUNE 28 🏵

If only I possessed the grace, good Jesus, to be utterly at one with you!
Amidst all the variety of worldly things around me, Lord, the only thing
I crave is unity with you. You are all my soul needs. Unite, dear friend of
my heart, this unique little soul of mine to your perfect goodness. You
are all mine; when shall I be yours? Lord Jesus, my beloved, be the
magnet of my heart; clasp, press, unite me for ever to your sacred heart.
You have made me for yourself; make me one with you. Absorb this tiny
drop of life into the ocean of goodness whence it came.

Francis de Sales, 1567–1622

JUNE 29

I love you, O my God, and my only desire is to love you until the last breath of my life. I love you, and I would rather die loving you, than live without loving you. I love you, Lord, and the only grace I ask is to love you eternally. My God, if my tongue cannot say in every moment that I love you, I want my heart to repeat it to you as often as I draw breath.

Jean-Baptiste Vianney, Curé d'Ars, 1786–1859

JUNE 30

In the evening of this life, I shall appear before you with empty hands, for I do not ask you, Lord, to count my works. All our goodness is stained and imperfect. I wish, then, to be clothed with your own goodness, and to receive you yourself eternally, out of your love. I want no other place or crown but you, my beloved.

Lord, even if my conscience were burdened with every sin it is possible to commit, I would still throw myself into your arms, my heart broken with contrition. And I know how tenderly you welcome any prodigal child of yours who comes back to you.

Thérèse of Lisieux, 1873–97

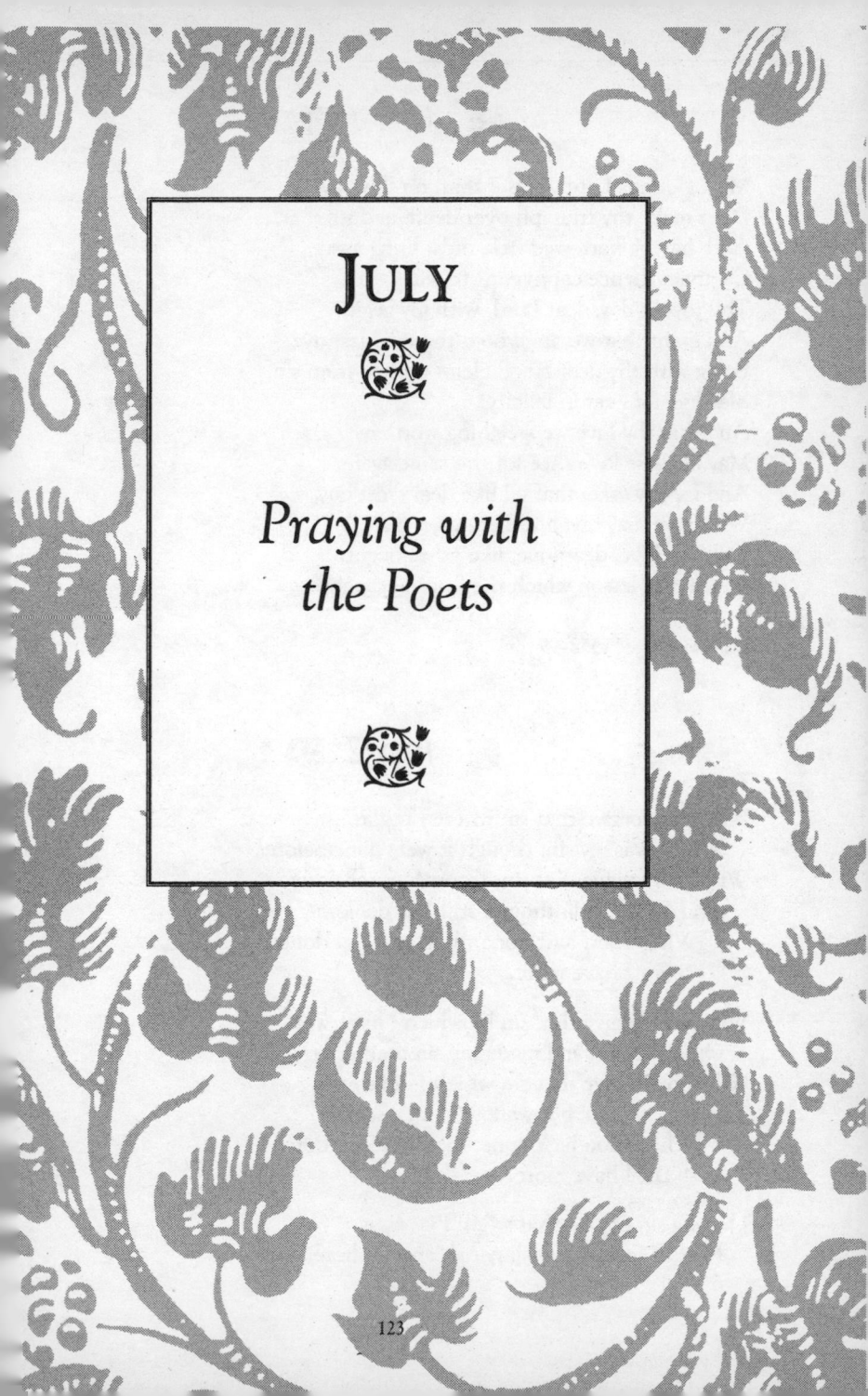

JULY

Praying with the Poets

🏵 JULY 1 🏵

Most glorious Lord of Life! that, on this day,
Didst make thy triumph over death and sin;
And, having harrowed hell, didst bring away
Captivity thence captive, us to win:
This joyous day, dear Lord, with joy begin;
And grant that we, for whom thou diddest dye,
Being with thy dear blood clean washed from sin,
May live for ever in felicity!
And that thy love we weighing worthily,
May likewise love thee for the same again;
And for thy sake, that all like dear didst buy,
With love may one another entertain!
So let us love, dear love, like as we ought,
Love is the lesson which the Lord us taught.

Edmund Spenser, 1552–99

🏵 JULY 2 🏵

Wilt thou forgive that sin where I begun,
    Which was my sin, though it were done before?
Wilt thou forgive that sin, through which I run,
    And do run still: though still I do deplore?
        When thou hast done, thou hast not done,
            For I have more.

Wilt thou forgive that sin by which I have won
    Others to sin, and made my sin their door?
Wilt thou forgive that sin which I did shun
    A year, or two; but wallowed in, a score?
        When thou hast done, thou hast not done,
            For I have more.

I have a sin of fear, that when I've spun
    My last thread, I shall perish on the shore;

Swear by thyself that at my death thy Son
   Shall shine—as he shines now, and heretofore;
And, having done that, thou hast done,
     I fear no more.

John Donne, 1573–1631

🌿 JULY 3 🌿

How fresh, O Lord, how sweet and clean
Are thy returns! ev'n as the flowers in spring;
To which, besides their own demean,
The late-past frosts tributes of pleasure bring.
Grief melts away
Like snow in May,
As if there were no such cold thing.

Who would have thought my shrivel'd heart
Could have recover'd greennesse? It was gone
Quite under ground; as flowers depart
To see their mother-root, when they have blown;
Where they together
All the hard weather,
Dead to the world, keep house unknown.

These are thy wonders, Lord of power,
Killing and quickning, bringing down to hell
And up to heaven in an houre;
Making a chiming of a passing-bell.
We say amisse,
This or that is:
Thy word is all, if we could spell.

O that I once past changing were,
Fast in thy Paradise, where no flower can wither!
Many a spring I shoot up fair,
Offring at heav'n, growing and groning thither:
Nor doth my flower

Want a spring-showre,
My sinnes and I joining together:

But while I grow in a straight line,
Still upwards bent, as if heav'n were mine own,
Thy anger comes, and I decline:
What frost to that? what pole is not the zone,
Where all things burn,
When thou dost turn,
And the least frown of thine is shown?

And now in age I bud again,
After so many deaths I live and write;
I once more smell the dew and rain,
And relish versing: O my onely light,
It cannot be
That I am he
On whom thy tempests fell all night.

These are thy wonders, Lord of love,
To make us see we are but flowers that glide:
Which when we once can finde and prove,
Thou hast a garden for us, where to bide.
Who would be more,
Swelling through store,
Forfeit their Paradise by their pride.

George Herbert, 1593–1633

❧ JULY 4 ❧

Hear me, O God!
   A broken heart
   Is my best part:
Use still thy rod
   That I may prove
   Therein thy love.

If thou hadst not
   Been stern to me,
   But left me free,
I had forgot
   Myself and thee.

For sin's so sweet,
   As minds ill-bent
   Rarely repent,
Until they meet
   Their punishment.

Who more can crave
   Than gav'st a son
To free a slave,
   First made of nought,
   With all since bought?

Sin, Death, and Hell
   His glorious Name
   Quite overcame,
Yet I rebel,
   And slight the same.

But I'll come in,
   Before my loss
   Me farther toss,
As sure to win
   Under his cross.

Ben Jonson, 1572–1637

🏵 JULY 5 🏵

Lord, by this sweet and saving sign,
Defend us from our foes and thine.

Jesus, by thy wounded feet,
   Direct our path aright:

Jesus, by thy nailed hands,
    Move ours to deeds of love:
Jesus, by thy pierced side,
    Cleanse our desires:
Jesus, by thy crown of thorns,
    Annihilate our pride:
Jesus, by thy silence,
    Shame our complaints:
Jesus, by thy parched lips,
    Curb our cruel speech:
Jesus, by thy closing eyes,
    Look on our sin no more:
Jesus, by thy broken heart,
    Knit ours to thee.

And by this sweet and saving sign,
Lord, draw us to our peace and thine.

Richard Crashaw, 1613–49 and others

🌺 JULY 6 🌺

If I have played the truant, or have here
Failed in my part; Oh! thou that art my dear,
My mild, my loving tutor, Lord and God,
Correct my errors gently with thy rod.
I know that faults will many here be found,
But where sin dwells, there let thy grace abound.

Robert Herrick, 1591–1674

🌺 JULY 7 🌺

Lord! when thou didst thy self undress
Laying by thy robes of glory,
To make us more, thou wouldst be less,
And becamest a woeful story.

To put on clouds instead of light,
And clothe the morning-star with dust,
Was a translation of such height
As, but in thee, was ne'r expressed;

Brave worms, and earth! that thus could have
A God enclosed within your cell,
Your maker pent up in a grave,
Life locked in death, heaven in a shell;

Ah, my dear Lord! what couldst thou spy
In this impure, rebellious clay,
That made thee thus resolve to die
For those that kill thee every day?

O what strange wonders could thee move
To slight thy precious blood, and breath!
Sure it was love, my Lord; for love
Is only stronger far than death.

Henry Vaughan, 1621–95

❧ JULY 8 ❧

Creator Spirit, by whose aid
The world's foundations first were laid,
Come visit every pious mind;
Come pour thy joys on humankind;
From sin and sorrow set us free,
And make thy temples worthy thee...

Plenteous of grace, descend from high,
Rich in thy sevenfold energy,
Thou strength of his almighty hand,
Whose power does heaven and earth command!
Proceeding Spirit, our defence,
Who dost the gift of tongues dispense,
And crown'st thy gift with eloquence!

Refine and purge our earthy parts;
But, O, inflame and fire our hearts!
Our frailties help, our vice control,
Submit the senses to the soul;
And when rebellious they are grown,
Then lay thy hand and hold them down.

Chase from our minds the infernal foe,
And peace, the fruit of love, bestow;
And lest our feet should step astray,
Protect and guide us in the way.

Make us eternal truths receive,
And practise all that we believe:
Give us thyself that we may see
The Father and the Son, by thee.

Immortal honour, endless fame,
Attend the Almighty Father's Name:
The Saviour Son be glorified,
Who for lost man's redemption died;
And equal adoration be,
Eternal Paraclete, to thee.

John Dryden, 1631–1700

🌼 JULY 9 🌼

Thou art my God, sole object of my love;
Not for hope of endless joys above;
Not for the fear of endless pains below,
Which they who love thee must not undergo.
For me, and such as me, thou deignst to bear
An ignominious cross, the nails, the spear;
A thorny crown transpierced thy sacred brow,
While bloody sweats from every member flow.
For me in tortures thou resignst thy breath,
Embraced me on the cross, and saved me by death.
And can these sufferings fail my heart to move?

Such as then was, and is, thy love to me,
Such is, and shall be still, my love to thee—
To thee, Redeemer! mercy's sacred spring!
My God, my Father, Maker, and my King!

Alexander Pope, 1688–1744

❧ JULY 10 ❧

My spirit longeth for thee,
　Within my troubled breast;
Although I be unworthy
　Of so divine a guest.

Of so divine a guest,
　Unworthy though I be;
Yet has my heart no rest,
　Unless it comes from thee.

Unless it comes from thee,
　In vain I look around:
In all that I can see,
　No rest is to be found.

No rest is to be found,
　But in thy blessed love;
O, let my wish be crowned,
　And send it from above.

John Byrom, 1692–1763

❧ JULY 11 ❧

Hark, my soul! It is the Lord;
'Tis thy Saviour, hear his word;
Jesus speaks, and speaks to thee:
'Say, poor sinner, lov'st thou me?

'I delivered thee when bound,
And, when wounded, healed thy wound;
Sought thee wandering, set thee right,
Turned thy darkness into light.

'Can a woman's tender care
Cease towards the child she bare?
Yes, she may forgetful be,
Yet will I remember thee.

'Mine is an unchanging love,
Higher than the heights above;
Deeper than the depths beneath,
Free and faithful, strong as death.

'Thou shalt see my glory soon,
When the work of grace is done;
Partner of my throne shalt be:
Say, poor sinner, lov'st thou me?'

Lord, it is my chief complaint
That my love is weak and faint;
Yet I love thee and adore,
Oh for grace to love thee more!

William Cowper, 1731–1800

🕮 JULY 12 🕮

Lord:
How do I love thee? Let me count the ways.
I love thee to the depth and breadth and height
my soul can reach, when feeling out of sight
for the ends of being and of ideal grace.
I love thee to the level of every day's
most quiet need, by sun and candlelight.
I love thee freely, as men strive for right;
I love thee purely, as they turn from praise.

I love thee with a passion put to use
in my old griefs, and with my childhood faith.
I love thee with a love I seemed to lose
with my lost saints—I love thee with the breath,
smiles, tears, of all my life!
And, God, if thou dost choose
I shall love thee better after death.

Elizabeth Browning, 1806–61 (adapted)

JULY 13

Wilt thou not visit me?
The plant beside me feels thy gentle dew,
And every blade of grass I see
From thy deep earth its quickening moisture drew.

Wilt thou not visit me?
Thy morning calls on me with cheering tone;
And every hill and tree
Lend but one voice—the voice of thee alone.

Come, for I need thy love,
More than the flower the dew or grass the rain;
Come, gently as thy holy dove;
And let me in thy sight rejoice to live again.

I will not hide from them
When thy storms come, though fierce may be their wrath,
But bow with leafy stem,
And strengthened follow on thy chosen path.

Yes, thou wilt visit me:
Nor plant nor tree thine eye delights so well,
As, when from sin set free,
My spirit loves with thine in peace to dwell.

Jones Very, 1813–80

🌟 JULY 14 🌟

Oh blessed Lord! How much I need
Thy light to guide me on my way!
So many hands, that, without heed,
Still touch thy wounds and make them bleed,
So many feet that day by day
Still wander from thy fold astray!
Feeble at best is my endeavour!
I see but cannot reach the height
That lies for ever in the Light;
And yet for ever and for ever,
When seeming just within my grasp,
I feel my feeble hands unclasp,
And sink discouraged into night;
For thine own purpose thou has sent,
The strife and the discouragement.

Henry Wadsworth Longfellow, 1807–82

🌟 JULY 15 🌟

Tie the strings to my life, my Lord,
    Then I am ready to go!
Just a look at the horses—
    Rapid! That will do!

Put me in on the firmest side,
    So I shall never fall;
For we must ride to the Judgment,
    And it's partly down hill.

But never I mind the bridges
    And never I mind the sea;
Held fast in everlasting race
    By my own choice and thee.

Good-by to the life I used to live,
    And the world I used to know;

And kiss the hills for me, just once;
    Now I am ready to go!

Emily Dickinson, 1830–86

🌼 JULY 16 🌼

Therefore to whom turn I but to thee, the ineffable Name?
Builder and maker, thou, of houses not made with hands!
What, have fear of change from thee who art ever the same?
Doubt that thy power can fill the heart that thy power expands?
There shall never be one lost good! What was, shall live as before;
The evil is null, is nought, is silence implying sound;
What was good shall be good, with, for evil, so much good more;
On the earth the broken arcs; in the heaven, a perfect round.

All we have willed or hoped or dreamed of good shall exist;
Not its semblance, but itself; no beauty, nor good, nor power
Whose voice has gone forth, but each survives for the melodist
When eternity affirms the conception of an hour.
The high that proved too high, the heroic for earth too hard,
The passion that left the ground to lose itself in the sky,
Are music sent up to God by the lover and the bard;
Enough that he heard it once: we shall hear it by-and-by.

Robert Browning, 1812–89

🌼 JULY 17 🌼

Glory be to God for dappled things—
for skies of couple-colour as a brinded cow;
For rose-moles all in stipple upon trout that swim;
Fresh-firecoal chestnut-falls; finches' wings;
Landscape plotted and pierced-fold, fallow, and plough;
And all trades, their gear and tackle and trim.

All things counter, original, spare, strange;
Whatever is fickle, freckled (who knows how?)
With swift, slow; sweet, sour; adazzle, dim;
He fathers-forth whose beauty is past change:
Praise him.

Gerard Manley Hopkins, 1844–89

🟦 JULY 18 🟦

Strong Son of God, immortal Love,
    Whom we, that have not seen thy face,
    By faith, and faith alone, embrace,
Believing where we cannot prove;

Thine are these orbs of light and shade;
    Thou madest life in man and brute;
    Thou madest death; and lo, thy foot
Is on the skull which thou hast made.

Thou wilt not leave us in the dust:
    Thou madest man, he knows not why,
    He thinks he was not made to die;
And thou hast made him: thou art just.

Thou seemest human and divine,
    The highest, holiest manhood, thou:
    Our wills are ours, we know not how;
Our wills are ours, to make them thine.

Our little systems have their day;
    They have their day and cease to be:
    They are but broken lights of thee,
And thou, O Lord, art more than they.

Alfred, Lord Tennyson, 1809–92

JULY 19

O thou transcendent,
Nameless, the fibre and the breath,
Light of the light, shedding forth universes, thou centre of them,
Thou mightier centre of the true, the good, the loving,
Thou moral, spiritual fountain—affection's source—thou reservoir,
(O pensive soul of me—O thirst unsatisfied—waitest not there?
Waitest not haply for us somewhere there the Comrade perfect?)
Thou pulse—thou motive of the stars, suns, systems,
That, circling, move in order, safe, harmonious,
Athwart the shapeless vastnesses of space,
How should I think, how breathe a single breath, how speak, if,
    out of myself,
I could not launch, to those, superior universes?

Walt Whitman, 1819–92

JULY 20

O God the Holy Ghost
    who art light unto thine elect,
Evermore enlighten us.
Thou who art fire of love,
Evermore enkindle us.
Thou who art Lord and giver of life,
Evermore live in us.
Thou who bestowest sevenfold grace,
Evermore replenish us.
As the wind is thy symbol,
So forward our goings.
As the dove,
So launch us heavenwards.
As water,
So purify our spirits.
As a cloud,
So abate our temptations.

As dew,
So revive our languor.
As fire,
So purge out our dross.

Christina Rossetti, 1830–94

🏵 JULY 21 🏵

Come down, O Christ, and help me! reach thy hand,
   For I am drowning in a stormier sea
   Than Simon on thy lake of Galilee:
The wine of life is spilt upon the sand,
My heart is in some famine-murdered land
   Whence all good things have perished utterly,
   And well I know my soul in hell must lie
If I this night before God's throne should stand.
'He sleeps perchance, or rideth to the chase,
   Like Baal, when his prophets howled that name
   From morn to noon on Carmel's smitten height.'
Nay, peace, I shall behold, before the night,
   The feet of brass, the robe more white than flame,
The wounded hands, the weary human face.

Oscar Wilde, 1854–1900

🏵 JULY 22 🏵

   Thou art the Way
Hadst thou been nothing but the goal
   I cannot say
If thou hadst ever met my soul.

   I cannot see—
I, child of process—if there lies
   An end for me
Full of repose, full of replies.

I'll not reproach
The road that winds, my feet that err.
Access, Approach
Art thou, Time, Way, and Wayfarer.

Alice Meynell, 1847–1922

🌸 JULY 23 🌸

Eternal Father, who didst all create,
In whom we live, and to whose bosom move,
To all men be thy name known, which is love,
Till its loud praises sound at heaven's high gate.
Perfect thy kingdom in our passing state,
That here on earth thou mays't as well approve
Our service, as thou ownest theirs above,
Whose joy we echo and in pain await.

Grant body and soul each day their daily bread:
And should in spite of fresh grace woe begin,
Even as our anger soon is past and dead
Be thy remembrance mortal of our sin:
By thee in paths of peace thy sheep be led,
And in the vale of terror comforted.

Robert Bridges, 1844–1930

🌸 JULY 24 🌸

It is a fearful thing to fall into the hands of the living God.
But it is a much more fearful thing to fall out of them.

Did Lucifer fall through knowledge?
oh then, pity him, pity him that plunge!

Save me, O God, from falling into the ungodly knowledge
of myself as I am without God.
Let me never know, O God

let me never know what I am or should be
when I have fallen out of your hands, the hands of the living God.

That awful and sickening endless sinking, sinking
through the slow, corruptive levels of disintegrative knowledge
when the self has fallen from the hands of God,
and sinks, seething and sinking, corrupt
and sinking still, in depth after depth of disintegrative consciousness
sinking in the endless undoing, the awful katabolism into the abyss!
Even of the soul, fallen from the hands of God!

Save me from that, O God!
Let me never know myself apart from the living God!

D.H. Lawrence, 1885–1930

🕮 JULY 25 🕮

Non nobis Domine!—
  Not unto us, O Lord!
The praise or glory be
  Of any deed or word;
 For in thy judgment lies
  To crown or bring to nought
All knowledge or device
  That man has reached or wrought.

And we confess our blame—
  How all too high we hold
That noise which men call fame,
  That dross which men call gold.
For these we undergo
  Our hot and godless days,
But in our hearts we know
  Not unto us the praise.

O Power by whom we live—
  Creator, Judge, and Friend,
Upholdingly forgive
  Nor fail us at the end:

But grant us well to see
    In all our piteous ways—
Non nobis Domine!—
    Not unto us the praise!

Rudyard Kipling, 1885–1936

🕮 JULY 26 🕮

i thank You God for most this amazing
day:for the leaping greenly spirits of trees
and a blue true dream of sky;and for everything
which is natural which is infinite which is yes

(i who have died am alive again today,
and this is the sun's birthday;this is the birth
day of life and of love and wings:and of the gay
great happening illimitably earth)

how should tasting touching hearing seeing
breathing any—lifted from the no
of all nothing—human merely being
doubt unimaginable You?

(now the ears of my ears awake and
now the eyes of my eyes are opened)

e.e. cummings, 1894–1962

🕮 JULY 27 🕮

We praise thee, O God, for thy glory displayed in all the creatures of
    the earth,
In the snow, in the rain, in the wind, in the storm; in all of thy creatures,
    both the hunters and the hunted.
For all things exist only as seen by thee, only as known by thee, all
    things exist

Only in thy light, and thy glory is declared even in that which denies
thee; the darkness declares the glory of light.

Those who deny thee could not deny, if thou didst not exist; and their
denial is never complete, for if it were so, they would not exist.

They affirm thee in living; all things affirm thee in living; the bird in the
air, both the hawk and the finch; the beast on the earth, both the
wolf and the lamb; the worm in the soil and the worm in the belly.

T.S. Eliot, 1888–1965

🏵 JULY 28 🏵

O Christ who holds the open gate,
O Christ who drives the furrow straight,
O Christ, the plough, O Christ, the laughter
Of holy white birds flying after,
Lo, all my heart's field red and torn,
And thou wilt bring the young green corn
The young green corn divinely springing,
The young green corn forever singing,
And when the field is fresh and fair
Thy blessed feet shall glitter there
And we will walk the weeded field,
And tell the golden harvest's yield,
The corn that makes the holy bread
By which the soul of man is fed,
The holy bread, the food unpriced,
Thy everlasting mercy, Christ.

John Masefield, 1878–1967

🏵 JULY 29 🏵

I am not God's little lamb
I am God's sick tiger.
And I prowl about at night

And what most I love I bite,
And upon the jungle grass I slink,
Snuff the aroma of my mental stink,
Taste the salt tang of tears upon the brink
Of my uncomfortable muzzle.
My tail my beautiful, my lovely tail,
Is warped.
My stripes are matted and my coat once sleek
Hangs rough and undistinguished on my bones,
O God I was so beautiful when I was well.
My heart, my lungs, my sinews and my reins
Consumed a solitary ecstasy,
And light and pride informed each artery.
Then I a temple, now a charnel house.
Then I a high hozannah, now a dirge.
Then I a recompense of God's endeavour,
Now a reproach and earnest of lost toil.
Consider, Lord, a tiger's melancholy
And heed a minished tiger's muted moans,
For thou art sleek and shining bright
And I am weary.
Thy countenance is full of light
And mine is dreary.

Stevie Smith, 1902–71

🕸 JULY 30 🕸

We have had names for you:
The Thunderer, the Almighty
Hunter, Lord of the snowflake
and the sabre-toothed tiger.
One name we have held back
unable to reconcile it
with the mosquito, the tidal wave,
the black hole into which
time will fall. You have answered

us with the image of yourself
on a hewn tree, suffering
injustice, pardoning it;
pointing as though in either
direction; horrifying us
with the possibility of dislocation.
Ah, love, with your arms out
wide, tell us how much more
they must still be stretched
to embrace a universe drawing
away from us at the speed of light.

R.S. Thomas

🌸 JULY 31 🌸

Whether I kneel or stand or sit in prayer,
I am not caught in time nor held in space,
but thrust beyond this posture I am where
time and eternity come face to face;
infinity and space meet in this place
where crossbar and high upright hold the one
in agony and in all Love's embrace.
The power in helplessness that was begun
when all the brilliance of the flaming sun
contained itself in the small confines of a child
now comes to me in this strange action done
in mystery. Break me, break space, O wild
and lovely power. Break me: thus am I dead,
am resurrected now in wine and bread.

Madeleine L'Engle

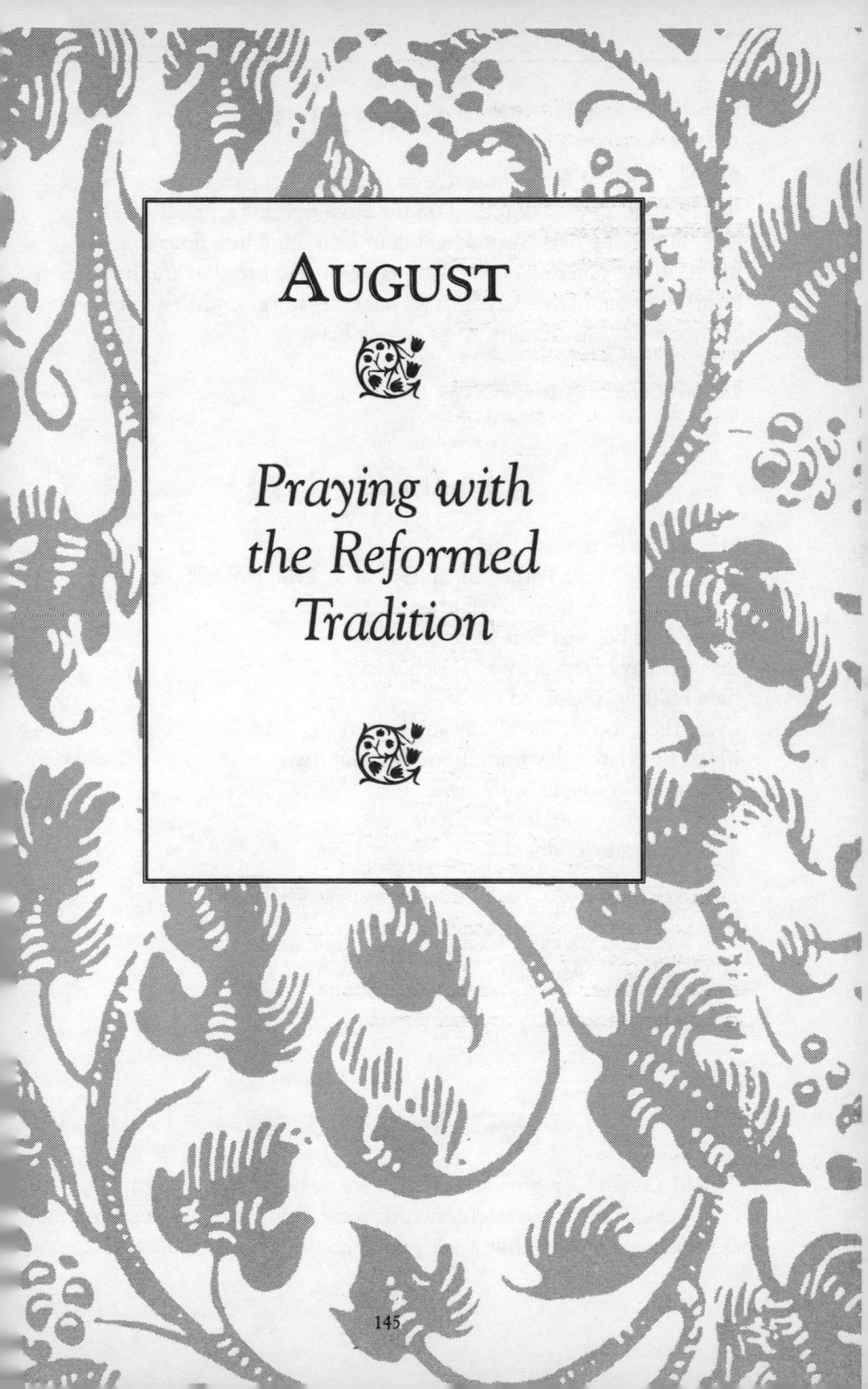

AUGUST

Praying with the Reformed Tradition

🏵 AUGUST 1 🏵

Just as a grain of wheat must die in the earth in order to bring forth a rich harvest, so your Son died on the cross to bring a rich harvest of love. Just as the harvest of wheat must be ground into flour to make bread, so the suffering of your Son brings us the bread of life. Just as bread gives our bodies strength for our daily work, so the risen body of your Son gives us strength to obey your laws.

Thomas Münzer, c. 1490–1525

🏵 AUGUST 2 🏵

I lay me down to rest,
in the name of the Father, of the Son and of the Holy Ghost.
I thank thee, my heavenly Father,
by thy dear beloved Son Jesus Christ,
that this day of thy plenteous rich mercy
thou has thus preserved me.
I pray thee, forgive me all my sins
which I have this day unrighteously committed
in deed, in word and in thought.
And that thou wouldst vouchsafe
of thy gracious goodness,
to keep me this night;
for I commit myself
both body and soul and all mine,
Into thy hands. Amen.

The Prymer of 1539

🏵 AUGUST 3 🏵

Behold, Lord, an empty vessel that needs to be filled. My Lord, fill it. I am weak in the faith; strengthen thou me. I am cold in love; warm me and make me fervent that my love may go out to my neighbour. I do not have a strong and firm faith; at times I doubt and am unable to trust thee altogether. O Lord, help me. Strengthen my faith and trust in thee. In thee I have sealed the treasure of all I have. I am poor; thou art rich and didst come to be merciful to the poor. I am a sinner; thou art upright. With me, there is an abundance of sin, in thee is the fullness of righteousness.

Therefore I will remain with thee of whom I can receive, but to whom I may not give.

Amen.

Martin Luther, 1483–1546

🌼 AUGUST 4 🌺

O heavenly Father, the author and fountain of all truth, the bottomless sea of all understanding, send, we beseech thee, thy Holy Spirit into our hearts, and lighten our understandings with the beams of thy heavenly grace. We ask this, O merciful Father, for thy dear Son, our Saviour, Jesus Christ's sake.

Nicholas Ridley, c. 1500–55

🌼 AUGUST 5 🌺

O thou who in almighty power wast weak, and in perfect excellency wast lowly, grant unto us the same mind. All that we have which is our own is naught; if we have any good in us it is wholly thy gift. O Saviour, since thou, the Lord of heaven and earth, didst humble thyself, grant unto us true humility, and make us like thyself; and then, of thine infinite goodness, raise us to thine everlasting glory; who livest and reignest with the Father and the Holy Ghost for ever and ever.

Thomas Cranmer, 1489–1556

🌑 AUGUST 6 🌑

Almighty and Holy Spirit, the comforter, pure, living, true—illuminate, govern, sanctify me, and confirm my heart and mind in the faith, and in all genuine consolation; preserve and rule over me that, dwelling in the house of the Lord all the days of my life, to behold the beauty of the Lord, I may be and remain forever in the temple of the Lord, and praise him with a joyful spirit, and in union with all the heavenly Church.

Philip Melanchthon, 1497–1560

🌑 AUGUST 7 🌑

Give ear, O Lord, unto our prayer,
and attend to the voice of our supplication.
Make us poor in spirit: that ours may be the kingdom of heaven.
Make us to mourn for sin: that we may be comforted by thy grace
Make us meek: that we may inherit the earth.
Make us to hunger and thirst after righteousness:
    that we may be filled therewith.
Make us merciful: that we may obtain mercy.
Make us pure in heart: that we may see thee.
Make us peacemakers: that we may be called thy children.
Make us willing to be persecuted for righteousness' sake:
    that our reward may be great in heaven.

Book of Common Order, 1562

🌑 AUGUST 8 🌑

O merciful God, eternal light, shining in darkness, thou who dispellest the night of sin and all blindness of heart, since thou hast appointed the night for rest and the day for labour, we beseech thee grant that our bodies may rest in peace and quietness, that afterward they may be able to endure the labour they must bear.

Temper our sleep that it be not disorderly, that we may remain spotless both in body and soul, yea that our sleep itself may be to thy glory.

Enlighten the eyes of our understanding that we may not sleep in death, but always look for deliverance from this misery.

Defend us against all assaults of the devil and take us into thy holy protection.

And although we have not passed this day without greatly sinning against thee, we beseech thee to hide our sins with thy mercy, as thou hidest all things on earth with the darkness of the night, that we may not be cast out from thy presence.

Relieve and comfort all those who are afflicted in mind, body, or estate. Through Jesus Christ our Lord.

John Calvin, 1509–64

❧ AUGUST 9 ❧

Most loving Saviour,
it is written in thy holy gospel,
that thou camest into this world,
not to call the righteous, but sinners, to repentance.
Suffer me not, O Lord,
to be of the number of those
who justify themselves
who, boasting their own righteousness,
their own works and merits,
despise the righteousness that cometh by faith,
which alone is allowable before thee.
Give me grace to know and acknowledge myself as I am,
even the son of wrath by nature;
a wretched sinner, and unprofitable servant,
and wholly to depend on thy merciful goodness
with strong and unshaken faith,
that in this world thou mayest continually call me
unto true repentance; seeing I continually sin,

and in the world to come
bring me unto everlasting glory.

Thomas Becon, c. 1513–67

🏵 AUGUST 10 🏵

O God, give us patience when those who are wicked hurt us. O how
impatient and angry we are when we think ourselves unjustly slandered,
reviled and hurt! Christ suffers blows upon his cheek, the innocent for
the guilty; yet we may not abide one rough word for his sake. O Lord,
grant us virtue and patience, power and strength, that we may take all
adversity with goodwill, and with a gentle mind overcome it. And if
necessity and thy honour require us to speak, grant that we may do so
with meekness and patience, that the truth and thy glory may be
defended, and our patience and steadfast continuance perceived.

Miles Coverdale, 1488–1568

🏵 AUGUST 11 🏵

What was it that Paul received of the Lord?
God, of his mercy open our hearts:
to see our errors, and content ourselves
to be ordered by the wisdom of God,
to do that God will have us to do,
to believe that God will have us to believe,
to worship that God will have us worship.
So shall we have comfort of the holy mysteries;
so shall we receive the fruits of Christ's death;
so shall we be partakers of Christ's body and blood;
so shall Christ truly dwell in us,
and we in him.
So shall all error be taken from us;
so shall we join all together in God's truth;

so shall we all be able,
with one heart and one spirit,
to know and to glorify
the only, the true, and the living God,
and his only-begotten Son Jesus Christ;
to whom both with the Holy Ghost
be all honour and glory
For ever and ever.

John Jewel, 1522–71

August 12

O God of all power, who hast called from death the great pastor of the sheep, our Lord Jesus: comfort and defend the flock which he hath redeemed by the blood of the eternal testament. Increase the number of true preachers; lighten the hearts of the ignorant; relieve the pains of such as be afflicted, especially of those that suffer for the testimony of the truth; by the power of our Lord Jesus Christ.

John Knox, 1505–72

August 13

What shall befall us hereafter we know not; but to God, who cares for all men, who will one day reveal the secrets of all hearts, we commit ourselves wholly, with all who are near and dear to us. And we beseech the same most merciful and almighty God, that for the time to come we may so bear the reproach of Christ with unbroken courage, as ever to remember that here we have no continuing city, but may seek one to come, by the grace and mercy of our Lord Jesus Christ; to whom with the Father, and the Holy Ghost, be all honour and dominion, world without end.

Matthew Parker, 1504–75

❧ AUGUST 14 ❧

O Lord God, when thou givest to thy servants to endeavour any great matter, grant us also to know that it is not the beginning, but the continuing of the same to the end, until it be thoroughly finished, which yieldeth the true glory; through him who for the finishing of thy work laid down his life, our Redeemer, Jesus Christ.

Sir Francis Drake, 1541–96

❧ AUGUST 15 ❧

Lord, give us hearts never to forget thy love; but to dwell therein whatever we do, whether we sleep or wake, live or die, or rise again to the life that is to come. For thy love is eternal life and everlasting rest; for this is life eternal to know thee and thy infinite goodness. O let its flame never be quenched in our hearts; let it grow and brighten, till our whole souls are glowing and shining with its light and warmth. Be thou our joy, our hope, our strength and life, our shield and shepherd, our portion for ever. For happy are we if we continue in the love wherewith thou hast loved us; holy are we when we love thee steadfastly. Therefore, O thou, whose name and essence is love, enkindle our hearts, enlighten our understanding, sanctify our wills, and fill all the thoughts of our hearts, for Jesus Christ's sake.

Johann Arndt, 1555–1621

❧ AUGUST 16 ❧

As I take off my dusty, dirty clothes, let me also be stripped of the sins I have committed this day. I confess, dear Lord, that in so many ways my thoughts and actions have been impure. Now I come before you, naked in body and bare in soul, to be washed clean. Let me rest tonight in your arms, and so may the dreams that pass through my mind be holy. And let me awake tomorrow, strong and eager to serve you.

Jakob Boehme, 1575–1624

❧ AUGUST 17 ❧

Strengthen us, O God, to relieve the oppressed, to hear the groans of poor prisoners, to reform the abuses of all professions; that many be made not poor to make a few rich; for Jesus Christ's sake.

Oliver Cromwell, 1599–1658

❧ AUGUST 18 ❧

We humbly beseech thee, of thy goodness, O Lord, to comfort and succour all them who in this transitory life are in trouble, sorrow, need, sickness, or any other adversity: help us to minister to them thy strength and consolation, and so endow us with the grace of sympathy and compassion that we may bring to them both help and healing; through Jesus Christ our Lord.

Book of Common Prayer, 1662

❧ AUGUST 19 ❧

He that is down needs fear no fall
He that is low, no pride:
He that is humble ever shall
Have God to be his guide.

I am content with what I have,
Little be it or much:
And, Lord, contentment still I crave,
Because thou savest such.

John Bunyan, 1628–88

❧ AUGUST 20 ❧

Keep me, O Lord, while I tarry on this earth, in a daily serious seeking after thee, and in a believing affectionate walking with thee; that, when thou comest, I may be found not hiding my talent, nor serving my flesh, nor yet asleep with my lamp unfurnished; but waiting and longing for my Lord, my glorious God, for ever and ever.

Richard Baxter, 1615–91

❧ AUGUST 21 ❧

O Lord, lift up the light of your countenance upon us; let your peace rule in our hearts, and may it be our strength and our song in the house of our pilgrimage. We commit ourselves to your care and keeping; let your grace be mighty in us, and sufficient in us, for all the duties of the day. Keep us from sin. Give us the rule over our own spirits, and guard us from speaking unadvisedly with our lips. May we live together in holy love and peace, and do you command your blessing upon us, even life for evermore.

Matthew Henry, 1662–1714

❧ AUGUST 22 ❧

We give them back to thee, dear Lord, who gavest them to us. Yet as thou didst not lose them in giving, so we have not lost them by their return. What thou gavest thou takest not away, O Lover of souls; for what is thine is ours also if we are thine. And life is eternal and love is immortal, and death is only an horizon, and an horizon is nothing save the limit of our sight. Lift us up, strong Son of God, that we may see further; cleanse our eyes that we may see more clearly; and draw us closer to thyself that we may know ourselves to be nearer to our loved ones who are with thee. And while thou dost prepare for us, prepare us also for that happy place, that where they are and thou art, we too may be for evermore.

William Penn, 1644–1718

❧ AUGUST 23 ❧

God, I give you the praise for days well spent. But I am yet unsatisfied, because I do not enjoy enough of you. I apprehend myself at too great a distance from you. I would have my soul more closely united to you by faith and love.

You know Lord that I would love you above all things. You made me, you know my desires, my expectations. My joys all centre in you and it is you that I desire. It is your favour, your acceptance, the communications of your grace that I earnestly wish for more than anything in the world.

I rejoice in your essential glory and blessedness. I rejoice in my relation to you, that you are my Father, my Lord and my God. I thank you that you have brought me so far. I will beware of despairing of your mercy for the time which is yet to come, and will give you the glory of your free grace.

Susanna Wesley, 1669–1742

❧ AUGUST 24 ❧

O Lord, my God! the amazing horrors of darkness were gathered round me, and covered me all over, and I saw no way to go forth; I felt the depth and extent of the misery of my fellow-creatures separated from the divine harmony, and it was heavier than I could bear, and I was crushed down under it; I lifted up my hand, I stretched out my arm, but there was none to help me; I looked round about, and was amazed.

In the depths of misery, O Lord, I remembered that thou art omnipotent; that I had called thee Father; and I felt that I loved thee, and I was made quiet in my will, and I waited for deliverance from thee. Thou hadst pity upon me, when no man could help me; I saw that meekness under suffering was showed to us in the most affecting example of thy Son, and thou taughtest me to follow him, and I said: 'Thy will, O Father, be done!'

John Woolman, 1720–72

🏵 AUGUST 25 🏵

Forgive them all, O Lord:
our sins of omission and our sins of commission;
the sins of our youth and the sins of our riper years;
the sins of our souls and the sins of our bodies;
our secret and our more open sins;
our sins of ignorance and surprise,
and our more deliberate and presumptuous sin;
the sins we have done to please ourselves
and the sins we have done to please others;
the sins we know and remember,
and the sins we have forgotten;
the sins we have striven to hide from others
and the sins by which we have made others offend;
forgive them, O Lord, forgive them all for his sake,
who died for our sins and rose for our justification,
and now stands at thy right hand to make intercession for us,
Jesus Christ our Lord.

John Wesley, 1703–91

🏵 AUGUST 26 🏵

O God, from whom we have received life, and all earthly blessings,
vouchsafe to give unto us each day what we need. Give unto all of us
strength to perform faithfully our appointed tasks; bless the work of our
hands and of our minds. Grant that we may ever serve thee, in sickness
and in health, in necessity and in abundance; sanctify our joys and our
trials, and give us grace to seek first thy kingdom and its righteousness,
in the sure and certain faith that all else shall be added unto us; through
Jesus Christ, thy Son, our Lord and Saviour.

Eugene Bersier, 1831–89

AUGUST 27

O my Saviour,
let me not fall by little and little,
or think myself able to bear
the indulgence of any known sin
because it seems so insignificant.
Keep me from sinful beginnings,
lest they lead me on
to sorrowful endings.

Charles Haddon Spurgeon, 1834–92

AUGUST 28

Use me, then, my Saviour, for whatever purpose, and in whatever way, thou may require. Here is my poor heart, an empty vessel; fill it with thy grace. Here is my sinful and troubled soul; quicken it and refresh it with thy love. Take my heart for thine abode; my mouth to spread abroad the glory of thy name; my love and all my powers, for the advancement of your believing people; and never suffer the steadfastness and confidence of my faith to abate; so that at all times I may be enabled from the heart to say, 'Jesus needs me, and I am his.'

Dwight L. Moody, 1837–99

AUGUST 29

O God our Father, help us to a deeper trust in the life everlasting. May we feel that this love which is now, ever shall be; this robe of the flesh is thy gift to thy child, and, when it is worn out, thou wilt clothe him again; this work of life is the work thou hast given us to do, and, when it is done, thou wilt give us more; this love, that makes all our life so glad, flows from thee, for thou art love, and we shall love forever. Help us to feel how, day by day, we see some dim shadow of the eternal day that will break upon us at the last. May the gospel of thy Son, the whisper of thy Spirit, unite to make our faith in the life to come, strong and clear; then shall we be glad when thou shalt call us, and enter into thy glory in Jesus Christ.

Robert Collyer, 1823–1912

❧ AUGUST 30 ❧

My Father in heaven, I remember those
whom in prayer I am inclined to forget.
I pray for those whom I dislike.
Defend me against my own feelings;
change my inclinations;
give me a compassionate heart.
Give me, I pray, the purity of heart
which finds your image in all people.

J.H. Jowett, 1846–1923

❧ AUGUST 31 ❧

Through every minute of this day,
Be with me, Lord!
Through every day of all this week
Be with me, Lord!
Through every week of all this year
Be with me, Lord!
Through all the years of all this life,
Be with me, Lord!
So shall the days and weeks and years
Be threaded on a golden cord.
And all draw on with sweet accord
Unto thy fullness, Lord
That so, when time is past,
By grace I may at last,
Be with thee, Lord.

John Oxenham, 1862–1941

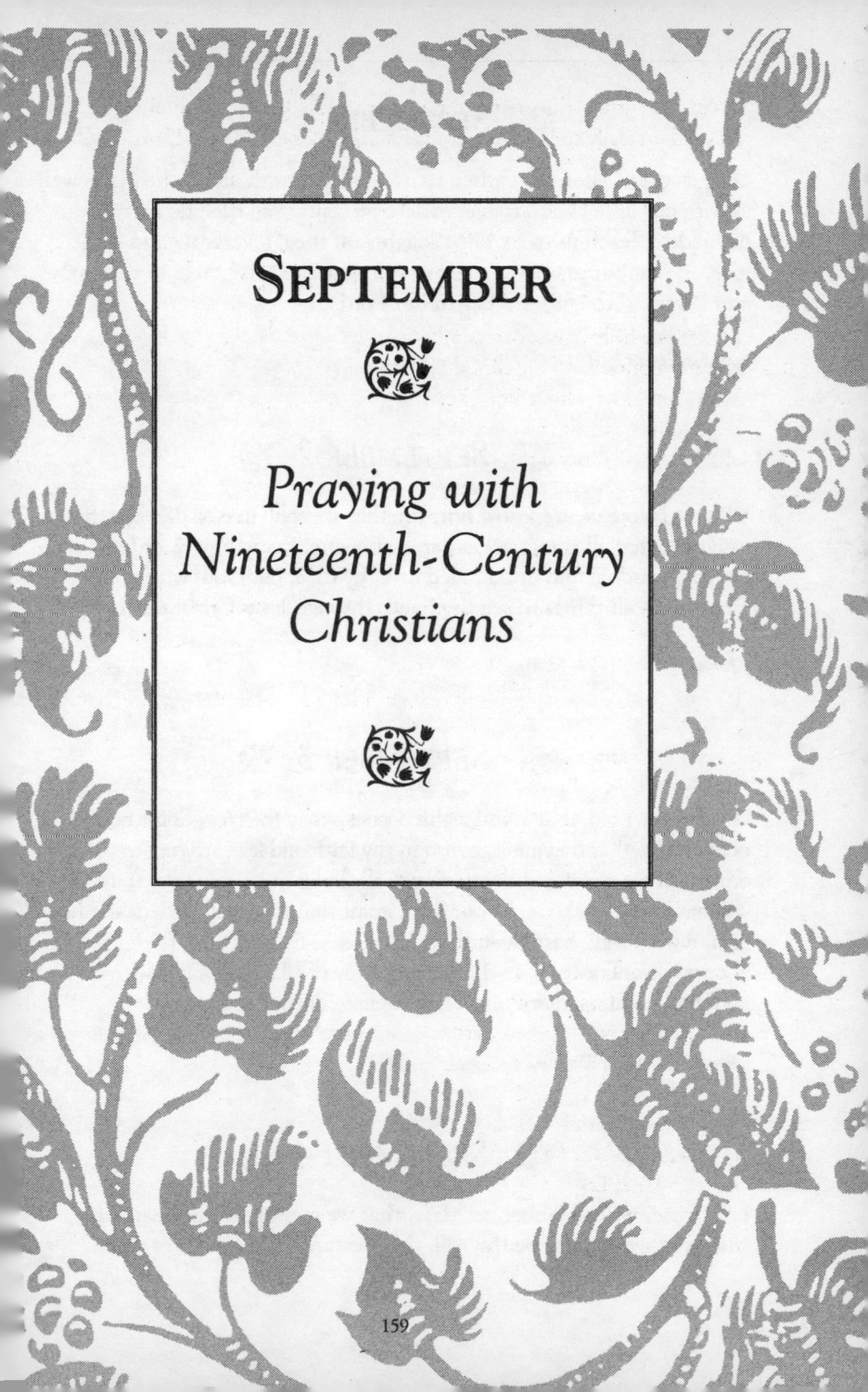

SEPTEMBER

Praying with Nineteenth-Century Christians

SEPTEMBER 1

Give us grace, almighty Father, to address thee with all our hearts as well as with our lips. Thou art everywhere present: from thee no secrets can be hidden. Teach us to fix our thoughts on thee, reverently and with love, so that our prayers are not in vain, but are acceptable to thee, now and always; through Jesus Christ our Lord.

Jane Austen, 1775–1817

SEPTEMBER 2

What is before us, we know not, whether we shall live or die; but this we know, that all things are ordered and sure. Everything is ordered with unerring wisdom and unbounded love, by thee, our God, who art love. Grant us in all things to see thy hand; through Jesus Christ our Lord.

Charles Simeon, 1759–1836

SEPTEMBER 3

O righteous Lord, that lovest righteousness, may thy Holy Spirit be with our rulers... that they may govern in thy faith and fear, striving to put down all that is evil and to encourage all that is good. Give thy spirit of wisdom to those who make our laws, grant that they may understand how great a work thou hast given them to do; that they may not do it lightly, but gravely and soberly, to the putting away of all wrong and oppression and to the advancement of the true welfare of thy people.

Thomas Arnold, 1795–1842

SEPTEMBER 4

Lord, teach us to number our days, that we may apply our hearts unto wisdom. Lighten, if it be thy will, the pressures of this world's cares.

Above all, reconcile us to thy will, and give us a peace which the world cannot take away; through Jesus Christ our Lord.

Thomas Chalmers, 1780–1847

🏵 SEPTEMBER 5 🏵

No coward soul is mine,
No trembler in the world's storm-tossed sphere:
I see heaven's glories shine,
And faith shines equal, arming me from fear.

O God within my breast,
Almighty, ever-present Deity!
Life—that in me has rest,
As I—undying Life—have power in thee!

Vain are the thousand creeds
That move men's hearts: unutterably vain;
Worthless as withered weeds,
Or idlest froth amid the boundless main,

To waken doubt in one
Holding so fast by thine infinity;
So surely anchored on
The steadfast rock of immortality.

With wide-embracing love
Thy spirit animates eternal years,
Pervades and broods above,
Changes, sustains, dissolves, creates, and rears.

Though earth and man were gone,
And suns and universes ceased to be,
And thou were left alone,
Every existence would exist in thee.

There is not room for Death,
Nor atom that his might could render void:

Thou—THOU art Being and Breath,
And what THOU art may never be destroyed.

Emily Brontë, 1818–48

🌼 SEPTEMBER 6 🌼

While faith is with me, I am blest;
It turns my darkest night to day;
But, while I clasp it to my breast,
I often feel it slide away.

What shall I do if all my love,
My hopes, my toil, are cast away?
And if there be no God above
To hear and bless me when I pray?

Oh, help me, God! For thou alone
Canst my distracted soul relieve.
Forsake it not: it is thine own,
Though weak, yet longing to believe.

Anne Brontë, 1820–49

🌼 SEPTEMBER 7 🌼

Father in heaven! You speak to us in many ways. Even when you are
silent, you still speak to us, in order to examine us, to try us, and so that
the hour of our understanding may be more profound.

Oh, in the time of silence, when I remain alone and abandoned
because I do not hear your voice, it seems as if the separation must last
for ever. Father in heaven! It is only a moment of silence in the intimacy
of a conversation. Bless then this silence, and let me not forget that you
are silent through love, and that you speak through love, so that in your
silence and in your word you are still the same Father, and that you guide
and instruct even by your silence.

Søren Kierkegaard, 1813–55

❧ SEPTEMBER 8 ❧

O God, who hast made of one blood all nations of men for to dwell on the face of the earth, and didst send thy blessed Son, Jesus Christ, to preach peace to them that are afar off, and to them that are nigh; grant that all the peoples of the world may feel after thee and find thee; hasten, O God, the fulfilment of thy promise to pour out thy spirit upon all flesh, through Jesus Christ our Lord.

George Cotton, 1813–66

❧ SEPTEMBER 9 ❧

O Lord, grant me to greet the coming day in peace. Help me in all things to rely upon thy holy will. In every hour of the day reveal thy will to me. Bless my dealings with all who surround me. Teach me to treat all that comes to me throughout the day with peace of soul, and with firm conviction that thy will governs us all. In all my deeds and words guide my thoughts and feelings. In unforeseen events let me not forget that all are sent by thee. Teach me to act firmly and wisely, without embittering and embarrassing others. Give me strength to bear the fatigue of thy coming day with all that it shall bring. Direct my will, teach me to pray, pray thou thyself in me.

Drizdov Philaret, 1782–1867

❧ SEPTEMBER 10 ❧

O Lord, give us more charity, more self-denial, more likeness to thee. Teach us to sacrifice our comforts to others, and our likings for the sake of doing good. Make us kindly in thought, gentle in word, generous in deed. Teach us that it is better to give than to receive, better to forget ourselves than to put ourselves forward, better to minister than to be ministered unto. And to thee, the God of love, be all glory and praise, now and for ever.

Henry Alford, 1810–71

❧ SEPTEMBER 11 ❧

We let the world overcome us; we live too much in continual fear of the chances and changes of mortal life. We let things go too much their own way. We try too much to get what we can by our own selfish wits, without considering our neighbour. We follow too much the ways and fashions of the day, doing and saying and thinking anything that comes uppermost, just because there is so much around us. Free us from our selfish interests, and guide us, good Lord, to see thy way and to do thy will.

Charles Kingsley, 1819–75

❧ SEPTEMBER 12 ❧

O most merciful Saviour, we come to offer thee the incense of worshipping hearts. We come as those who by faith behold him that is invisible. We speak to thee as simply as if our bodily eyes saw thee, as if thou wert openly seated in the midst of us, and thy hand were visibly outstretched to give the gift we ask. We thank thee for thy mercies, for the safety and rest of the night, for the hopes and the duties of the day. We cannot know what the day will bring, but we know that it will bring most surely thy love and grace for thy people, and continual opportunities of doing thy will and giving ourselves up to thy use. Knowing thee, we know all we need to know of the unknown future, near or far away. May this day, then, be a day of holy peace and happiness in our home and in each heart. If it pleases thee, keep us from all accident and illness and evil tidings. But, above all, fill us from within with that holy calm which circumstances can neither give nor take away, for it is thyself dwelling and ruling in us. May we recollect and realize thy presence, not at another time only, but today, and in the secret power of it may we meet in peace the common things of life as they come, all calls to act and think for others, all crossings of our wills, all pains and joys. Let nothing take us unawares, inasmuch as we are found in thee; for thine own name's sake.

H.G.C. Moule, 1801–80

❧ SEPTEMBER 13 ❧

Teach me, O Father, how to ask thee each moment, silently, for thy help.
If I fail, teach me at once to ask thee to forgive me. If I am disquieted,
enable me, by thy grace, quickly to turn to thee. May nothing this day
come between me and thee. May I will, do, and say, just what thou, my
loving and tender Father, willest me to will, do, and say. Work thy holy
will in me and through me this day. Protect me, guide me, bless me,
within and without, that I may do something this day for love of thee;
something which shall please thee; and that I may, this evening, be
nearer to thee, though I see it not, nor know it. Lead me, O Lord, in a
straight way unto thyself, and keep me in thy grace unto the end.

Edward Bouverie Pusey, 1800–82

❧ SEPTEMBER 14 ❧

O God, the father of the forsaken, the help of the weak, the supplier of the
needy; you teach us that love towards the race of man is the bond of
perfectness, and the imitation of your blessed self. Open and touch our
hearts that we may see and do, both for this world and that which is to
come, the things that belong to our peace. Strengthen us in the work
which we have undertaken; give us wisdom, perseverance, faith, and zeal,
and in your own time and according to your pleasure prosper the issue; for
the love of your Son Jesus Christ.

Lord Shaftesbury, 1801–85

❧ SEPTEMBER 15 ❧

Dear Jesus, help us to spread your fragrance everywhere we go. Flood our
souls with your spirit and life. Penetrate and possess our whole being so
utterly that our lives may only be a radiance of yours. Shine through us,
and be so in us, that every soul we come in contact with may feel your
presence in our soul. Let them look up and see no longer us but only
Jesus! Stay with us, and then we shall begin to shine as you shine; so to

share as to be a light to others; the light, O Jesus, will be all from you, none of it will be ours; it will be you, shining on others through us. Let us preach you without preaching, not by words but by our example, by the catching force, the sympathetic influence of what we do, the evident fullness of the love our hearts bear to you.

John Henry Newman, 1801–90

🌼 SEPTEMBER 16 🌼

O thou Lord of all worlds, we bless thy name for all those who have entered into their rest, and reached the promised land where thou art seen face to face. Give us grace to follow in their footsteps, as they followed in the footsteps of thy holy Son. Keep alive in us the memory of those dear to ourselves whom thou hast called to thyself; and grant that every remembrance which turns our hearts from things seen to things unseen may lead us always upwards to thee, till we come to our eternal rest; through Jesus Christ our Lord.

Fenton John Anthony Hort, 1828–92

🌼 SEPTEMBER 17 🌼

Lord, receive our supplications for this house, family and country. Protect the innocent, restrain the greedy and the treacherous, lead us out of our tribulation into a quiet land.

Look down upon ourselves and our absent dear ones. Help us and them, prolong our days in peace and honour. Give us health, food, bright weather and light hearts. In what we meditate of evil, frustrate our wills; in what of good, further our endeavours. Cause injuries to be forgotten and benefits to be remembered. Let us lie down without fear and awake and arise with exultation. For his sake, in whose words we now conclude, Amen.

Robert Louis Stevenson, 1850–94

SEPTEMBER 18

Set before our minds and hearts, O heavenly Father, the example of our Lord Jesus Christ, who, when he was upon earth, found his refreshment in doing the will of him that sent him, and in finishing his work. When many are coming and going, and there is little leisure, give us grace to remember him who knew neither impatience of spirit nor confusion of work, but in the midst of all his labours held communion with thee, and even upon earth was still in heaven; where now he reigneth with thee and the Holy Spirit world without end.

Charles Vaughan, 1816–97

SEPTEMBER 19

Most loving Father, who willest us to give thanks for all things, to dread nothing but the loss of thee, and to cast all our care on thee who carest for us: preserve us from faithless fears and worldly anxieties, and grant that no clouds of this mortal life may hide us from the light of thy love which is immortal, and which thou has manifested to us in thy Son, Jesus Christ our Lord.

William Bright, 1824–1901

SEPTEMBER 20

Almighty God who hast sent the Spirit of truth unto us to guide us into all truth: so rule our lives by thy power that we may be truthful in thought and word and deed. May no fear or hope ever make us false in act or speech; cast out from us whatsoever loveth or maketh a lie, and bring us all into the perfect freedom of thy truth; through Jesus Christ our Lord.

Brooke Foss Westcott, 1825–1901

❧ SEPTEMBER 21 ❧

In times of doubts and questionings, when our belief is perplexed by new learning, new teaching, new thought, when our faith is strained by creeds, by doctrines, by mysteries beyond our understanding, give us the faithfulness of learners and the courage of believers in thee; give us boldness to examine and faith to trust all truth; patience and insight to master difficulties; stability to hold fast our tradition with enlightened interpretation to admit all fresh truth made known to us, and in times of trouble, to grasp new knowledge readily and to combine it loyally and honestly with the old; alike from stubborn rejection of new revelations, and from hasty assurance that we are wiser than our fathers,

Save us and help us, we humbly beseech thee, O Lord.

George Ridding, 1828–1904

❧ SEPTEMBER 22 ❧

Lord, teach us to understand that your Son died to save us not from suffering but from ourselves, not from injustice, far less from justice, but from being unjust. He died that we might live—but live as he lives, by dying as he died who died to himself.

George MacDonald, 1824–1905

❧ SEPTEMBER 23 ❧

We thank thee, O Lord and master, for teaching us how to pray simply and sincerely to thee, and for hearing us when we so call upon thee. We thank thee for saving us from our sins and sorrows, and for directing all our ways this day. Lead us ever onwards to thyself; for the sake of Jesus Christ our Lord and Saviour.

Father John of the Russian Church, 1829–1909

❧ SEPTEMBER 24 ❧

I thank you, O God, for the pleasures you have given me through my
senses; for the glory of thunder, for the mystery of music, the singing of
birds and the laughter of children. I thank you for the delights of colour,
the awe of the sunset, the wild roses in the hedgerows, the smile of
friendship. I thank you for the sweetness of flowers and the scent of hay.
Truly, O Lord, the earth is full of your riches!

Edward King, 1829–1910 (adapted)

❧ SEPTEMBER 25 ❧

Almighty God, from whom all thoughts of truth and peace proceed,
kindle, we pray thee, in the hearts of all men the true love of peace,
and guide with thy pure and peaceable wisdom those who take counsel
for the nations of the earth; that in tranquillity thy kingdom may go
forward, till the earth be filled with the knowledge of thy love; through
Jesus Christ our Lord.

Francis Paget, 1851–1911

❧ SEPTEMBER 26 ❧

O God, who art everywhere present, look down with thy mercy upon
those who are absent from among us. Give thy holy angels charge over
them, and grant that they may be kept safe in body, soul and spirit, and
presented faultless before the presence of thy glory with exceeding joy;
through Jesus Christ our Lord.

Richard Meux Benson, 1824–1915

❧ SEPTEMBER 27 ❧

My Father, I abandon myself to you. Do with me as you will. Whatever you may do with me I thank you. I am prepared for anything. I accept everything, provided your will is fulfilled in me and in all creatures. I ask for nothing more, my God. I place my soul in your hands. I give it to you, my God, with all the love of my heart, because I love you. And for me it is a necessity of love, this gift of myself, this placing of myself in your hands without reserve in boundless confidence, because you are my Father.

Charles de Foucauld, 1858–1916

❧ SEPTEMBER 28 ❧

Pour into our hearts the spirit of unselfishness, so that, when our cup overflows, we may seek to share our happiness with our brethren. O thou God of love, who makest thy sun to rise on the evil and on the good, and sendest rain on the just and the unjust, grant that we may become more and more thy true children, by receiving into our souls more of thine own spirit of ungrudging and unwearying kindness; which we ask in the name of Jesus Christ.

John Hunter, 1849–1917

❧ SEPTEMBER 29 ❧

O God, we thank you for this earth, our home; for the wide sky and the blessed sun, for the salt sea and the running water, for the everlasting hills and the never-resting winds, for trees and the common grass underfoot.

We thank you for our senses by which we hear the songs of birds, and see the splendour of the summer fields, and taste of the autumn fruits, and rejoice in the feel of the snow, and smell the breath of the spring.

Grant us a heart wide open to all this beauty; and save our souls from being so blind that we pass unseeing when even the common thornbush is aflame with your glory, O God our creator, who lives and reigns for ever and ever.

Walter Rauschenbusch, 1861–1918

SEPTEMBER 30

All this day, O Lord,
let me touch as many lives as possible for thee;
and every life I touch, do thou by thy Spirit quicken,
whether through the word I speak,
the prayer I breathe, or the life I live.

Mary Sumner, 1828–1921

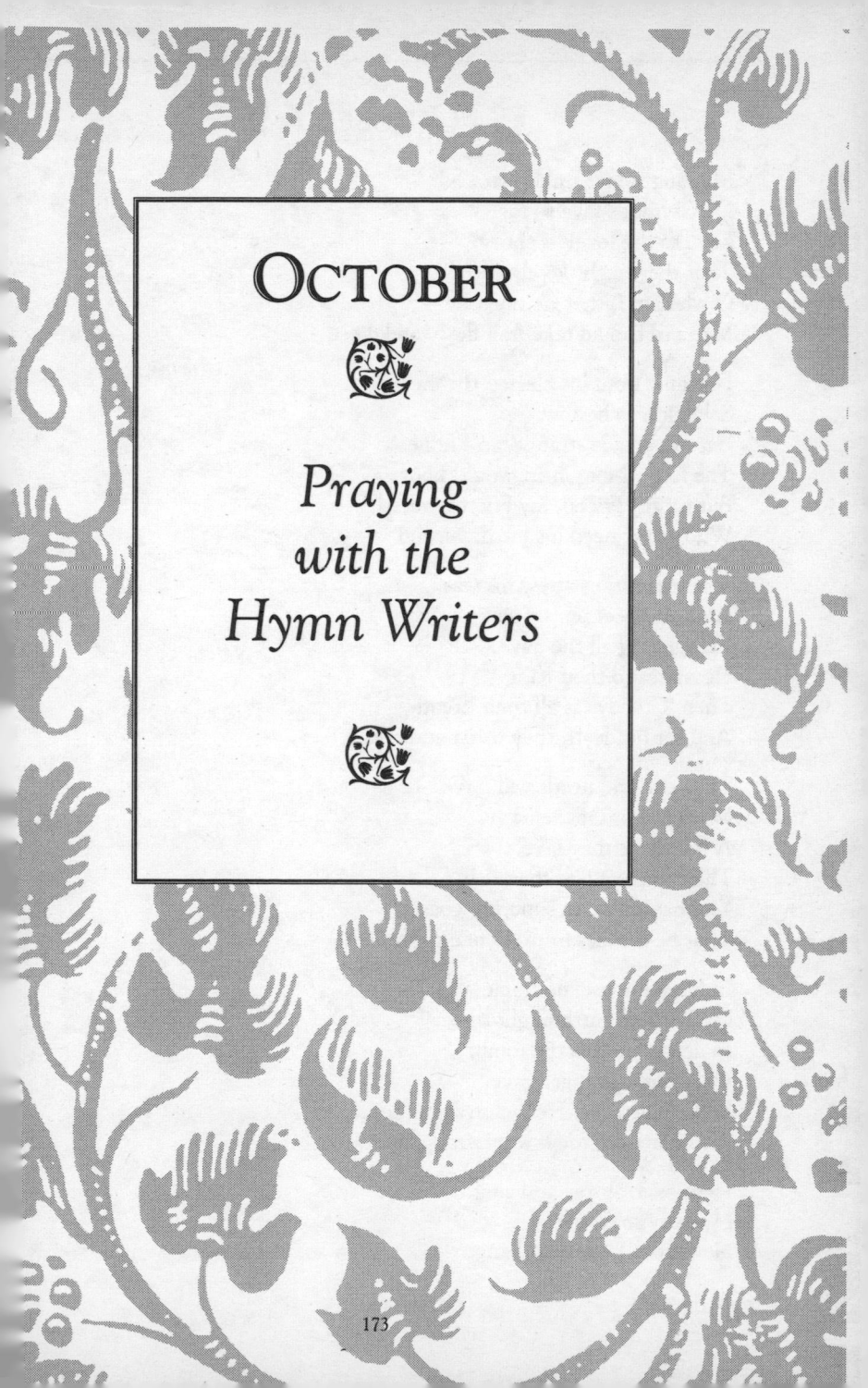

OCTOBER

*Praying
with the
Hymn Writers*

My song is love unknown,
My Saviour's love to me:
Love to the loveless shown,
That they might lovely be.
O who am I, that for my sake
My Lord should take frail flesh, and die?

He came from his blessed throne
Salvation to bestow;
But men made strange, and none
The longed-for Christ would know:
But O! my Friend, my Friend indeed,
Who at my need his life did spend.

Sometimes they strew his way,
And his sweet praises sing;
Resounding all the day
Hosannas to their King:
Then 'Crucify!' is all their breath,
And for his death they thirst and cry.

They rise and needs will have
My dear Lord made away;
A murderer they save,
The Prince of Life they slay,
Yet cheerful he to suffering goes,
That he his foes from thence might free.

In life no house, no home
My Lord on earth might have;
In death, no friendly tomb,
But what a stranger gave.
What may I say? Heaven was his home;
And mine the tomb wherein he lay.

Here might I stay and sing,
No story so divine,
Never was love, dear King!

Never was grief like thine.
This is my Friend, in whose sweet praise
I all my days could gladly spend.

Samuel Crossman, 1624–83

❦ OCTOBER 2 ❦

Glory to thee, my God, this night
For all the blessings of the light;
Keep me, O keep me, King of kings,
Under thy own almighty wings.

Forgive me, Lord, for thy dear Son,
The ill that I this day have done,
That with the world, myself, and thee,
I, e'er I sleep, at peace may be.

Teach me to live, that I may dread
The grave as little as my bed;
Teach me to die, that so I may
Triumphing rise at the last day.

O may my soul on thee repose,
And with sweet sleep mine eyelids close—
Sleep that may me more vigorous make
To serve my God when I awake.

When in the night I sleepless lie,
My soul with heavenly thoughts supply;
Let no ill dreams disturb my rest,
No powers of darkness me molest.

Praise God from whom all blessings flow,
Praise him, all creatures here below;
Praise him above, ye heavenly host,
Praise Father, Son, and Holy Ghost.

Thomas Ken, 1637–1711

OCTOBER 3

When I survey the wondrous cross,
On which the Prince of Glory died,
My richest gain I count but loss,
And pour contempt on all my pride.

Forbid it, Lord, that I should boast
Save in the death of Christ my God;
All the vain things that charm me most,
I sacrifice them to his blood.

See from his head, his hands, his feet,
Sorrow and love flow mingled down;
Did e'er such love and sorrow meet,
Or thorns compose so rich a crown?

His dying crimson, like a robe,
Spreads o'er his body on the tree;
Then am I dead to all the globe,
And all the globe is dead to me.

Were the whole realm of nature mine,
That were a present far too small;
Love so amazing, so divine,
Demands my soul, my life, my all.

Isaac Watts, 1674–1748

OCTOBER 4

Thou hidden Love of God, whose height,
Whose depth unfathomed, no man knows,
I see from far thy beauteous light,
Inly I sigh for thy repose;
My heart is pained, nor can it be
At rest, till it find rest in thee.

'Tis mercy all, that thou hast brought
My heart to seek for peace in thee;
Yet, while I seek but find thee not,
No peace my wandering mind shall see;
Oh, when shall all my wanderings end,
And all my steps to thee-ward tend?

Is there a thing beneath the sun
That strives with thee my heart to share?
Ah, tear it thence, and reign alone,
The Lord of every motion there!
Then shall my heart from pain be free,
When it hath found repose in thee.

O Lord! thy sovereign aid impart
To save me from low-thoughted care;
Chase this self-will through all my heart,
Through all its latent mazes there;
Make me thy duteous child, that I
Ceaseless may 'Abba Father', cry!

Gerhard Tersteegen, 1697–1769

🏵 OCTOBER 5 🏵

Love divine, all loves excelling,
Joy of heaven to earth come down,
Fix in us thy humble dwelling,
All thy faithful mercies crown.
Jesu, thou art all compassion,
Pure, unbounded love thou art;
Visit us with thy salvation,
Enter every trembling heart.

Come, almighty to deliver,
Let us all thy life receive;
Suddenly return, and never,
Never more thy temples leave.

Thee we would be always blessing,
Serve thee as thy hosts above,
Pray, and praise thee, without ceasing,
Glory in thy perfect love.

Finish then thy new creation,
Pure and spotless let us be;
Let us see thy great salvation,
Perfectly restored in thee.
Changed from glory into glory,
Till in heaven we take our place,
Till we cast our crowns before thee,
Lost in wonder, love, and praise!

Charles Wesley, 1707–88

🎕 OCTOBER 6 🎕

O Lord my God! when I in awesome wonder
Consider all the works thy hand hath made,
I see the stars, I hear the mighty thunder,
Thy pow'r throughout the universe display'd:
Then sings my soul, my Saviour God, to thee,
How great thou art! How great thou art!
Then sings my soul, my Saviour God, to thee,
How great thou art! How great thou art!

When through the woods and forest glades I wander
And hear the birds sing sweetly in the trees;
When I look down from lofty mountain grandeur,
And hear the brook, and feel the gentle breeze;
Then sings my soul, my Saviour God, to thee,
How great thou art! How great thou art!
Then sings my soul, my Saviour God, to thee,
How great thou art! How great thou art!

And when I think that God his Son not sparing,
Sent him to die—I scarce can take it in.

That on the cross my burden gladly bearing,
He bled and died to take away my sin:
Then sings my soul, my Saviour God, to thee,
How great thou art! How great thou art!
Then sings my soul, my Saviour God, to thee,
How great thou art! How great thou art!

When Christ shall come with shout of acclamation
And take me home—what joy shall fill my heart!
Then shall I bow in humble adoration
And there proclaim, my God, how great thou art!
Then sings my soul, my Saviour God, to thee,
How great thou art! How great thou art!
Then sings my soul, my Saviour God, to thee,
How great thou art! How great thou art!

Stuart K. Hine, based on a poem by Carl Boberg, 19th century

❦ OCTOBER 7 ❦

Amazing grace! how sweet the sound
That saved a wretch like me!
I once was lost, but now am found,
Was blind, but now I see.

'Twas grace that taught my heart to fear,
And grace my fears relieved;
How precious did that grace appear
The hour I first believed!

Through many dangers, toils, and snares
I have already come;
'Tis grace that brought me safe thus far
And grace will lead me home.

The Lord has promised good to me,
His word my hope secures;
He will my shield and portion be
As long as life endures.

Yes, when this heart and flesh shall fail
And mortal life shall cease
I shall possess within the veil
A life of joy and peace.

John Newton, 1725–1807

❧ OCTOBER 8 ❧

O worship the King all glorious above;
O gratefully sing his power and his love;
Our shield and defender, the Ancient of Days,
Pavilioned in splendour and girded with praise.

O tell of his might, O sing of his grace,
Whose robe is the light, whose canopy space;
His chariots of wrath the deep thunder clouds form,
And dark is his path on the wings of the storm.

The earth with its store of wonders untold,
Almighty, thy power hath founded of old;
Hath 'stablished it fast by a changeless decree,
And round it hath cast, like a mantle, the sea.

Thy bountiful care what tongue can recite?
It breathes in the air, it shines in the light;
It streams from the hills, it descends to the plain,
And sweetly distils in the dew and the rain.

Frail children of dust and feeble as frail,
In thee do we trust, nor find thee to fail;
Thy mercies how tender, how firm to the end!
Our maker, defender, redeemer, and friend.

O measureless might, ineffable love,
While angels delight to hymn thee above,
Thy humbler creation, though feeble their lays,
With true adoration shall sing to thy praise.

Robert Grant, 1779–1838

🌼 OCTOBER 9 🌼

Abide with me; fast falls the eventide;
The darkness deepens; Lord, with me abide;
When other helpers fail, and comforts flee,
Help of the helpless, O abide with me.

Swift to its close ebbs out life's little day;
Earth's joys grown dim, its glories pass away;
Change and decay in all around I see:
O thou who changest not, abide with me!

I need thy presence every passing hour,
What but thy grace can foil the tempter's power?
Who like thyself my guide and stay can be?
Through cloud and sunshine, O abide with me.

I fear no foe with thee at hand to bless;
Ills have no weight, and tears no bitterness.
Where is death's sting? where, grave, thy victory?
I triumph still, if thou abide with me.

Hold thou thy cross before my closing eyes,
Shine through the gloom, and point me to the skies;
Heaven's morning breaks, and earth's vain shadows flee:
In life, in death, O Lord, abide with me!

Henry Francis Lyte, 1793–1847

🌼 OCTOBER 10 🌼

Sun of my soul, thou Saviour dear,
It is not night if thou be near;
O may no earth-born cloud arise,
To hide thee from thy servant's eyes!

When the soft dews of kindly sleep
My wearied eyelids gently steep,
Be my last thought; how sweet to rest
For ever on my Saviour's breast!

Abide with me from morn till eve,
For without thee I cannot live;
Abide with me when night is nigh,
For without thee I dare not die.

If some poor wandering child of thine
Have spurned today the voice divine,
Now, Lord, the gracious work begin;
Let him no more lie down in sin.

Watch by the sick; enrich the poor
With blessings from thy boundless store;
Be every mourner's sleep tonight
Like infant's slumbers, pure and light.

Come near and bless us when we wake,
Ere through the world our way we take,
Till in the ocean of thy love
We lose ourselves in heaven above.

John Keble, 1792–1866

❅ OCTOBER 11 ❅

Lead us, heavenly Father, lead us
O'er the world's tempestuous sea;
Guard us, guide us, keep us, feed us,
For we have no help but thee;
Yet possessing every blessing
If our God our Father be.

Saviour, breathe forgiveness o'er us,
All our weakness thou dost know,
Thou didst tread this earth before us,
Thou didst feel its keenest woe;
Son of Mary, lone and weary,
Victor through this world didst go.

Spirit of our God, descending,
Fill our hearts with heavenly joy,

Love with every passion blending,
Pleasure that can never cloy:
Thus provided, pardoned, guided,
Nothing can our peace destroy.

James Edmeston, 1791–1867

🌸 OCTOBER 12 🌸

Just as I am, without one plea
But that thy blood was shed for me,
And that thou bid'st me come to thee,
O Lamb of God, I come, I come.

Just as I am, and waiting not
To rid my soul of one dark blot,
To thee, whose blood can cleanse each spot,
O Lamb of God, I come, I come.

Just as I am, though tossed about
With many a conflict, many a doubt,
Fightings and fears within, without,
O Lamb of God, I come, I come.

Just as I am, poor, wretched, blind;
Sight, riches, healing of the mind,
Yea, all I need, in thee to find,
O Lamb of God, I come, I come.

Just as I am, thou wilt receive,
Wilt welcome, pardon, cleanse, relieve,
Because thy promise I believe,
O Lamb of God, I come, I come.

Just as I am, thy love unknown
Has broken every barrier down;
Now to be thine, yea, thine alone,
O Lamb of God, I come, I come.

Just as I am, of that free love
The breadth, length, depth, and height to prove,
Here for a season, then above,
O Lamb of God, I come, I come.

Charlotte Elliott, 1789–1871

🏵 OCTOBER 13 🏵

Father and Friend, thy light, thy love
Beaming through all thy works we see;
Thy glory gilds the heavens above,
And all the earth is full of thee.

Thy voice we hear—thy presence feel,
Whilst thou, too pure for mortal sight,
Involved in clouds invisible,
Reignest the Lord of life and light.

We know not in what hallowed part
Of heaven's expanse thy throne may be;
But this we know, that where thou art
Strength, wisdom, goodness, dwell with thee.

Thy children shall not faint nor fear,
Sustained by this assuring thought—
Since thou, their God, art everywhere,
They cannot be where thou art not.

J. Bowring, 1792–1872

🏵 OCTOBER 14 🏵

O Jesus, I have promised
To serve thee to the end;
Be thou for ever near me,
My Master and my Friend;

I shall not fear the battle
If thou art by my side,
Nor wander from the pathway
If thou wilt be my Guide.

O let me feel thee near me;
The world is ever near;
I see the sights that dazzle,
The tempting sounds I hear;
My foes are ever near me,
Around me and within;
But Jesus, draw thou nearer,
And shield my soul from sin.

O let me hear thee speaking
In accents clear and still,
Above the storms of passion,
The murmurs of self-will;
O speak to reassure me,
To hasten, or control;
O speak, and make me listen,
Thou guardian of my soul.

O Jesus, thou hast promised
To all who follow thee
That where thou art in glory
There shall thy servants be;
And, Jesus, I have promised
To serve thee to the end;
O give me grace to follow
My Master and my Friend.

O let me see thy footmarks,
And in them plant mine own;
My hope to follow duly
Is in thy strength alone.
O guide me, call me, draw me,
Uphold me to the end;

And then in heaven receive me,
My Saviour and my Friend.

John Ernest Bode, 1816–74

❦ OCTOBER 15 ❦

Take my life, and let it be
Consecrated, Lord, to thee;
Take my moments and my days,
Let them flow in ceaseless praise.

Take my hands, and let them move
At the impulse of thy love.
Take my feet, and let them be
Swift and beautiful for thee.

Take my voice, and let me sing
Always, only, for my King;
Take my lips, and let them be
Filled with messages from thee.

Take my silver and my gold;
Not a mite would I withhold;
Take my intellect, and use
Every power as thou shalt choose.

Take my will, and make it thine:
It shall be no longer mine.
Take my heart; it is thine own:
It shall be thy royal throne.

Take my love; my Lord, I pour
At thy feet its treasure-store.
Take myself, and I will be
Ever, only, all, for thee.

Frances Ridley Havergal, 1836–79

Thy way, not mine, O Lord,
However dark it be:
Lead me by thine own hand,
Choose out the path for me.

The kingdom that I seek
Is thine: so let the way
That leads to it be thine,
Else I must surely stray.

Take thou my cup, and it
With joy or sorrow fill,
As best to thee may seem;
Choose thou my good and ill.

Not mine, not mine the choice
In things or great or small;
Be thou my guide, my strength,
My wisdom and my all.

Horatius Bonar, 1808–89

❦ OCTOBER 17 ❦

Breathe on me, Breath of God,
Fill me with life anew;
That I may love what thou dost love
And do what thou wouldst do.

Breathe on me, Breath of God,
Until my heart is pure;
Until my will is one with thine
To do and to endure.

Breathe on me, Breath of God,
Till I am wholly thine;
Until this earthly part of me
Glows with thy fire divine.

Breathe on me, Breath of God,
So shall I never die,
But live with thee the perfect life
Of thine eternity.

Edwin Hatch, 1835–89

❧ OCTOBER 18 ❧

Dear Lord and Father of mankind,
Forgive our foolish ways!
Re-clothe us in our rightful mind,
In purer lives thy service find,
In deeper reverence praise.

In simple trust like theirs who heard,
Beside the Syrian sea,
The gracious calling of the Lord,
Let us, like them, without a word
Rise up and follow thee.

O Sabbath rest by Galilee!
O calm of hills above,
Where Jesus knelt to share with thee
The silence of eternity,
Interpreted by love!

Drop thy still dews of quietness,
Till all our strivings cease;
Take from our souls the strain and stress,
And let our ordered lives confess
The beauty of thy peace.

Breathe through the hearts of our desire
Thy coolness and thy balm;
Let sense be dumb, let flesh retire;
Speak through the earthquake, wind, and fire,
O still small voice of calm!

John Greenleaf Whittier, 1807–92

OCTOBER 19

The day thou gavest, Lord, is ended,
The darkness falls at thy behest;
To thee our morning hymns ascended,
Thy praise shall sanctify our rest.

We thank thee that thy Church unsleeping,
While earth rolls onward into light,
Through all the world her watch is keeping,
And rests not now by day or night.

As o'er each continent and island
The dawn leads on another day,
The voice of prayer is never silent,
Nor dies the strain of praise away.

The sun that bids us rest is waking
Our brethren 'neath the western sky,
And hour by hour fresh lips are making
Thy wondrous doings heard on high.

So be it, Lord; thy throne shall never,
Like earth's proud empires, pass away;
Thy Kingdom stands, and grows for ever,
Till all thy creatures own thy sway.

John Ellerton, 1826–93

OCTOBER 20

Spirit of God, that moved of old
Upon the waters' darkened face,
Come, when our faithless hearts are cold,
And stir them with an inward grace.

Thou that art power and peace combined,
All highest strength, all purest love,
The rushing of the mighty wind,
The brooding of the gentle dove.

Come give us still thy powerful aid,
And urge us on, and keep us thine;
Nor leave the hearts that once were made
Fit temples for thy grace divine;

Nor let us quench thy sevenfold light;
But still with softest breathings stir
Our wayward souls, and lead us right,
O Holy Ghost, the comforter.

Cecil Frances Alexander, 1818–95

❧ OCTOBER 21 ❧

It is a thing most wonderful,
Almost too wonderful to be,
That God's own Son should come from heav'n
And die to save a child like me.

And yet I know that it is true;
He came to this poor world below,
And wept, and toiled, and mourned, and died,
Only because he loved us so.

I cannot tell how he could love
A child so weak and full of sin;
His love must be most wonderful,
If he could die my love to win.

It is most wonderful, to know
His love for me so free and sure;
But 'tis more wonderful to see
My love for him so faint and poor.

And yet I want to love thee, Lord;
O light the flame within my heart
And I will love thee more and more,
Until I see thee as thou art.

W.W. How, 1823–97

❦ OCTOBER 22 ❦

At even, ere the sun was set,
The sick, O Lord, around thee lay;
O in what divers pains they met!
O with what joy they went away!

Once more 'tis eventide, and we,
Oppressed with various ills, draw near;
What if thy form we cannot see?
We know and feel that thou art here.

O Saviour Christ, our woes dispel:
For some are sick, and some are sad,
And some have never loved thee well,
And some have lost the love they had;

And some have found the world is vain,
Yet from the world they break not free;
And some have friends who give them pain,
Yet have not sought a friend in thee;

And none, O Lord, have perfect rest,
For none are wholly free from sin;
And they who fain would serve thee best
Are conscious most of wrong within.

O Saviour Christ, thou too art man;
Thou hast been troubled, tempted, tried;
Thy kind but searching glance can scan
The very wounds that shame would hide.

Thy touch has still its ancient power,
No word from thee can fruitless fall;
Hear, in this solemn evening hour,
And in thy mercy heal us all.

Henry Twells, 1823–1900

OCTOBER 23

O love that wilt not let me go,
I rest my weary soul in thee:
I give thee back the life I owe,
That in thine ocean depths its flow
May richer, fuller be.

O light that followest all my way,
I yield my flickering torch to thee:
My heart restores its borrowed ray,
That in thy sunshine's blaze its day
May brighter, fairer be.

O joy that seekest me through pain,
I cannot close my heart to thee:
I trace the rainbow through the rain,
And feel the promise is not vain,
That morn shall tearless be.

O cross that liftest up my head,
I dare not ask to fly from thee:
I lay in dust life's glory dead,
And from the ground there blossoms red
Life that shall endless be.

George Matheson, 1842–1906

OCTOBER 24

Immortal, invisible, God only wise,
In light inaccessible hid from our eyes,
Most blessed, most glorious the Ancient of Days,
Almighty, victorious thy great name we praise.

Unresting, unhasting, and silent as light,
Nor wanting, nor wasting, thou rulest in might;
Thy justice like mountains high soaring above
Thy clouds which are fountains of goodness and love.

To all life thou givest, to both great and small;
In all life thou livest, the true life of all;
We blossom and flourish as leaves on the tree,
And wither and perish; but naught changeth thee.

Great Father of glory, pure Father of light,
Thine angels adore thee, all veiling their sight;
All laud we would render: O help us to see
'Tis only the splendour of light hideth thee.

Walter Chalmers Smith, 1824–1908

🌠 OCTOBER 25 🌠

Father, hear the prayer we offer:
Not for ease that prayer shall be,
But for strength, that we may ever
Live our lives courageously.

Not for ever in green pastures
Do we ask our way to be:
But by steep and rugged pathways
Would we strive to climb to thee.

Not for ever by still waters
Would we idly quiet stay;
But would smite the living fountains
From the rocks along our way.

Be our strength in hours of weakness,
In our wanderings be our guide;
Through endeavour, failure, danger,
Father, be thou at our side.

Let our path be bright or dreary,
Storm or sunshine be our share;
May our souls, in hope unweary,
Make thy work our ceaseless prayer.

Maria Willis, 1824–1908

For the beauty of the earth,
For the beauty of the skies,
For the love which from our birth
Over and around us lies,
Lord of all, to thee we raise
This our sacrifice of praise.

For the beauty of each hour
Of the day and of the night,
Hill and vale and tree and flower,
Sun and moon and stars of light:
Lord of all, to thee we raise
This our sacrifice of praise.

For the joy of human love,
Brother, sister, parent, child,
Friends on earth, and friends above,
Pleasures pure and undefiled:
Lord of all, to thee we raise
This our sacrifice of praise.

For each perfect gift of thine,
To our race so freely given,
Graces human and divine,
Flowers of earth and buds of heaven:
Lord of all, to thee we raise
This our sacrifice of praise.

For thy church which evermore
Lifteth holy hands above,
Offering up on every shore
Her pure sacrifice of love,
Lord of all, to thee we raise
This our sacrifice of praise.

F.S. Pierpoint, 1835–1917

❧ OCTOBER 27 ❧

Great is thy faithfulness, O God my Father,
There is no shadow of turning with thee;
Thou changest not, thy compassions they fail not;
As thou hast been thou for ever wilt be.
Great is thy faithfulness! Great is thy faithfulness!
Morning by morning new mercies I see;
All I have needed thy hand hath provided,
Great is thy faithfulness, Lord unto me!

Summer and winter, and springtime and harvest,
Sun, moon and stars in their courses above,
Join with all nature in manifold witness
To thy great faithfulness, mercy and love.
Great is thy faithfulness! Great is thy faithfulness!
Morning by morning new mercies I see;
All I have needed thy hand hath provided,
Great is thy faithfulness, Lord unto me!

Pardon for sin and a peace that endureth,
Thine own dear presence to cheer and to guide;
Strength for today and bright hope for tomorrow,
Blessings all mine, with ten thousand beside!
Great is thy faithfulness! Great is thy faithfulness!
Morning by morning new mercies I see;
All I have needed thy hand hath provided,
Great is thy faithfulness, Lord unto me!

Thomas O. Chisolm, 1866–1960

❧ OCTOBER 28 ❧

O God in heaven, whose loving plan
Ordained for us our parents' care,
And, from the time our life began,
The shelter of a home to share.

Our Father, on the homes we love
Send down thy blessing from above.

May young and old together find
In Christ the Lord of every day,
That fellowship our homes may bind
In joy and sorrow, work and play.
Our Father, on the homes we love
Send down thy blessing from above.

The sins that mar our homes forgive;
From all self-seeking set us free;
Parents and children, may we live
In glad obedience to thee.
Our Father, on the homes we love
Send down thy blessing from above.

O Father, in our homes preside,
Their duties shared as in thy sight;
In kindly ways be thou our guide,
On mirth and trouble shed thy light.
Our Father, on the homes we love
Send down thy blessing from above.

Hugh Martin, 1890–1964

🐝 OCTOBER 29 🐝

Lord of all power, I give you my will,
In joyful obedience your tasks to fulfil.
Your bondage is freedom, your service is song,
And, held in your keeping, my weakness is strong.

Lord of all wisdom, I give you my mind,
Rich truth that surpasses man's knowledge to find.
What eye has not seen and what ear has not heard
Is taught by your Spirit and shines from your Word.

Lord of all bounty, I give you my heart;
I praise and adore you for all you impart;
Your love to inspire me, your counsel to guide,
Your presence to cheer me, whatever betide.

Lord of all being, I give you my all;
If e'er I disown you I stumble and fall;
But, sworn in glad service your word to obey,
I walk in your freedom to the end of the way.

Jack C. Winslow, 1882–1974

❦ OCTOBER 30 ❦

Spirit of God, in all that's true I know you;
Yours is the light that shines through thoughts and words.
Forgive my mind, slow as it is to read you,
My mouth so slow to speak the truth you are.

Spirit of God, in beauty I behold you;
Yours is the loveliness of all that's fair.
Forgive my heart, slow as it is to love you,
My soul so slow to wonder at your grace.

Spirit of God, in all that's good I meet you;
Yours is the rightness in each deed of love.
Forgive my will, slow as it is to serve you,
My feet so slow to go, my hands to do.

Spirit of God, in Jesus Christ you find me;
In him you enter through the door of faith.
From deep within me take possession of me—
My will, my heart, my mind all matched to his.

Reginald T. Brooks, 1918–85

❧ OCTOBER 31 ❧

Here, Master, in this quiet place,
Where anyone may kneel,
I also come to ask for grace,
Believing you can heal.

If pain of body, stress of mind,
Destroys my inward peace,
In prayer for others may I find
The secret of release.

If self upon its sickness feeds
And turns my life to gall,
Let me not brood upon my needs,
But simply tell you all.

You never said 'You ask too much'
To any troubled soul.
I long to feel your healing touch—
Will you not make me whole?

But if the thing I most desire
Is not your way for me,
May faith, when tested in the fire,
Prove its integrity.

Of all my prayers, may this be chief:
Till faith is fully grown,
Lord, disbelieve my unbelief,
And claim me as your own.

Fred Pratt Green

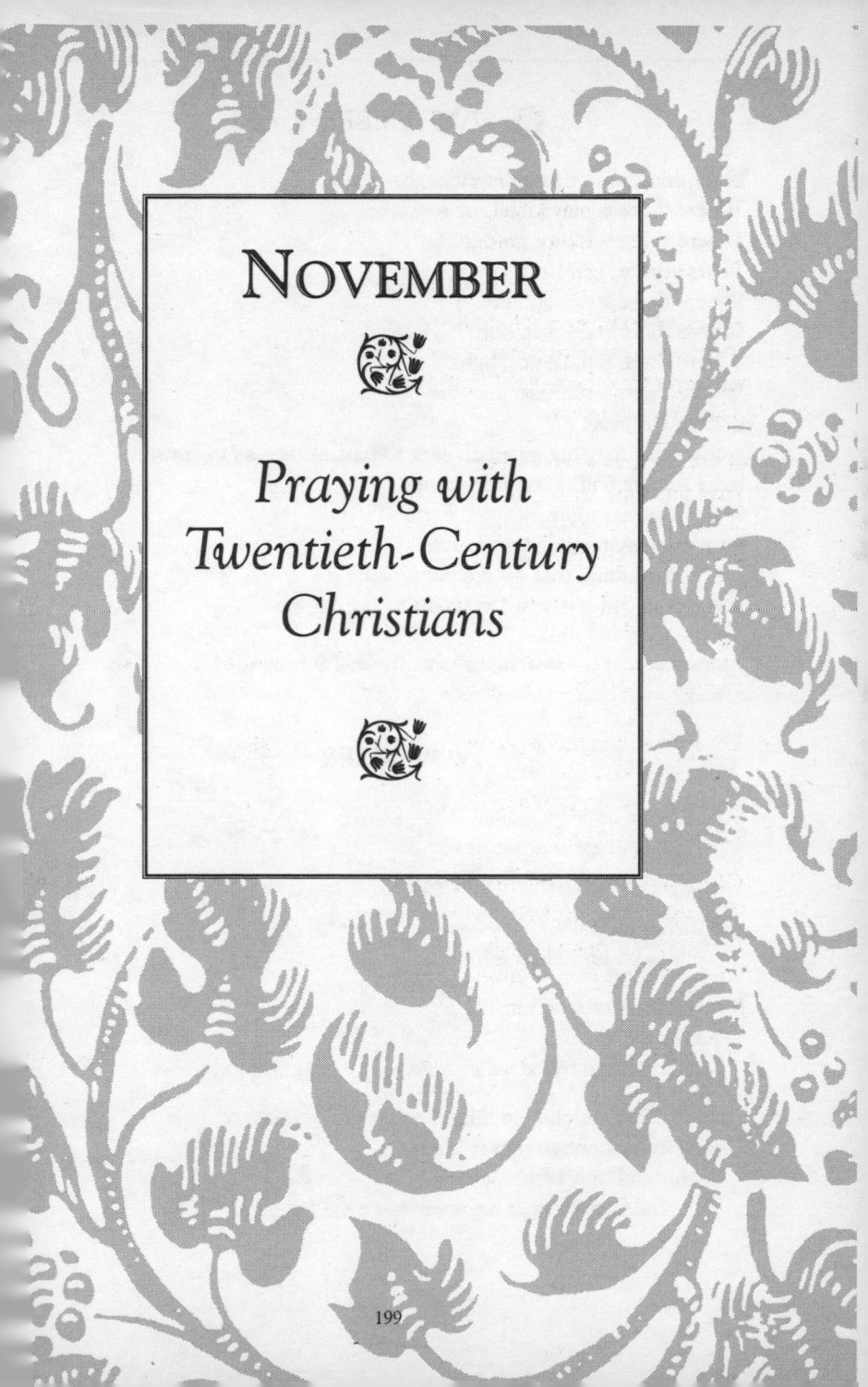

NOVEMBER

Praying with Twentieth-Century Christians

NOVEMBER 1

Lord, make me an instrument of thy peace.
Where there is hatred, let me sow love.
Where there is injury, pardon.
Where there is discord, vision.
Where there is doubt, faith.
Where there is despair, hope.
Where there is darkness, light.
Where there is sadness, joy.
O divine Master,
grant that I may not so much seek to be consoled as to console;
to be understood as to understand;
to be loved, as to love;
for it is in giving that we receive,
it is in pardoning that we are pardoned,
and it is in dying that we are born to eternal life.

Anonymous, c. 1913 (commonly called the Prayer of St Francis)

NOVEMBER 2

May he give us
   all the courage that we need
      to go the way he shepherds us.

That when he calls
   we may go unfrightened.

If he bids us come to him
   across the waters,
      that unfrightened we may go.

And if he bids us climb a hill,
   may we not notice that it is a hill,
      mindful only of
         the happiness of his company.

He made us for himself,
　　that we should travel with him
　　　　and see him at the last
　　　　　　in his unveiled beauty
　　　　　in the abiding city where
　　　　he is light
　　　　　and happiness
　　　　　　　and endless home.

Bede Jarrett, 1881–1934

🌸 NOVEMBER 3 🌸

The pinnacle of the Temple is a very lonely place.
You will not be waiting for me there.
Your method,
　　your prayer,
　　your disclosure of God,
　　take the lowliest path.
Your tabernacle among us is in the cave and the cottage.
I must come down like Zacchaeus
if I would have you dwell with me,
　　on the country roads of Galilee,
　　in the villages and on the shore,
　　down among the cares,
　　　　the sins,
　　　　labours
　　　　and sufferings of ordinary men—
there we shall find you.

'O teach me your ways
and hold up my going in your paths
that my footsteps slip not.'

Your paths are well-trodden.
Along them you and your saints have carried
healing and love
to ordinary men and women where they are.

Teach me to serve them as you serve—
    with patience,
    simplicity,
    reverence
    and love.

Your saints never presumed to grasp at
their spiritual privileges,
or use them for their own advantage:
nor sought extraordinary grace.
They loved to follow you along ordinary ways.
Help me to love those ways too.

Your spirit is not given that we may escape
life's friction and demands,
but so that we may live the common life
as you would have it lived—
in earth as in heaven.

Evelyn Underhill, 1875–1941

❦ NOVEMBER 4 ❦

O God of love, we pray thee to give us love:
Love in our thinking, love in our speaking,
Love in our doing, and love in the hidden places of our souls;
Love of our neighbours near and far;
Love of our friends, old and new;
Love of those with whom we find it hard to bear,
And love of those who find it hard to bear with us;
Love of those with whom we work,
And love of those with whom we take our ease;
Love in joy, love in sorrow;
Love in life and love in death;
That so at length we may be worthy to dwell with thee,
Who art eternal love.

William Temple, 1881–1944

❧ NOVEMBER 5 ❧

O God, early in the morning I cry to you. Help me to pray and to concentrate my thoughts on you; I cannot do this alone.

In me there is darkness, but with you there is light; I am lonely, but you do not leave me; I am feeble in heart, but with you there is help; I am restless, but with you there is peace.

In me there is bitterness, but with you there is patience; I do not understand your ways, but you know the way for me.

Dietrich Bonhoeffer, 1906–45

❧ NOVEMBER 6 ❧

O God, our Leader and our Master and our Friend, forgive our imperfections and our little motives, take us and make us one with thy great purpose, use us and do not reject us, make us all servants of thy kingdom, weave our lives into thy struggle to conquer and to bring peace and union to the world.

We are small and feeble creatures, we are feeble in speech, feebler still in action, nevertheless let but thy light shine upon us, and there is not one of us who cannot be lit by thy fire and who cannot lose himself in thy salvation. Take us into thy purposes, O God, let thy kingdom come into our hearts and into this world.

H.G. Wells, 1866–1946

❧ NOVEMBER 7 ❧

Think through me, thoughts of God;
My Father, quiet me,
Till in thy holy presence, hushed,
I think thy thoughts with thee.

Think through me, thoughts of God,
That always, everywhere,

The stream that through my being flows
May homeward pass in prayer.

Think through me, thoughts of God,
And let my own thoughts be
Lost like the sand-pools on the shore
Of the eternal sea.

Amy Carmichael, 1868–1951

❀ NOVEMBER 8 ❀

We confess before thee our blindness of heart, our poverty of life, our
littleness, our meanness, and our sin. We have not followed after Christ.
We have not given love to the loveless and the lost. Change thou our
lives, O God. Give us light that we may be light to those whose lives are
darkened. Give us life that we may be life-giving to the dying.

Help and uphold us when the temptations of the world press upon us.
Show us thy service. Open thy will to us, that we may serve thee aright.
Strengthen us when our hearts grow weak, and hope and faith flicker
and fail within us. Raise us when we fall; give us the power to stand, and
lend us the guiding light of thy cross, O Christ, to lead us home where
shadows are no more.

Lauchlan Maclean Watt, 1867–1957

❀ NOVEMBER 9 ❀

Teach us, O Father, to trust thee with life and with death,
And (though this is harder by far)
With the life and the death of those that are dearer to us
Than our life.

Teach us stillness and confident peace
In thy perfect will,
Deep calm of soul, and content
In what thou wilt do with these lives thou hast given.

Teach us to wait and be still,
To rest in thyself,
To hush this clamorous anxiety,
To lay in thine arms all this wealth thou hast given.

Thou lovest these souls that we love
With a love as far surpassing our own
As the glory of noon surpasses the gleam of a candle.

Therefore will we be still,
And trust in thee.

John S. Hoyland, 1887–1957

❁ NOVEMBER 10 ❁

God, let me put right before interest,
Let me put others before self,
Let me put the things of the spirit
before the things of the body.
Let me put the attainment of noble ends
above the enjoyment of present pleasures
Let me put principle above reputation.
Let me put thee before all else.

John Baillie, 1886–1960

❁ NOVEMBER 11 ❁

Great God, our Father: as we call to mind the scene of Christ's suffering
in Gethsemane, our hearts are filled with penitence and shame that we
foolishly waste our time in idleness and that we make no progress in the
Christian life from day to day… We are ashamed that war and lust
flourish and grow more rampant every day. Forgive us for our cruel
indifference to the cross, and pardon us that, like the bystanders of
old, we merely stand and gaze in idle curiosity upon the piteous scene.
O teach us, we beseech thee, the good news of thy forgiveness.

Cause humanity, degenerate as it is, to live anew, and hasten the day
when the whole world shall be born again.

Toyohiko Kagawa, 1888–1960

🥀 NOVEMBER 12 🥀

Thou who art over us,
Thou who art one of us,
Thou who art also within us,
May all see thee in me also,
May I prepare the way for thee,
May I thank thee for all that shall fall to my lot,
May I also not forget the needs of others,
Keep me in thy love
As thou wouldest that all should be kept in mine.
May everything in this my being be directed to thy glory
And may I never despair.
For I am under thy hand,
And in thee is all power and goodness.

Give me a pure heart—that I may see thee,
A humble heart—that I may hear thee,
A heart of love—that I may serve thee,
A heart of faith—that I may abide in thee.
To love life and men as God loves them—
    for the sake of their infinite possibilities,
        to wait like him
        to judge like him
        without passing judgment,
        to obey the order when it is given
        and never look back—
    then he can use you—then, perhaps, he will use you.
And if he doesn't use you—what matter. In his hand,
    every moment has its meaning, its greatness, its glory,
    its peace, its co-inherence.

Dag Hammarskjold, 1905–61

✿ NOVEMBER 13 ✿

O Jesus, Son of the living God, who became man and made the supreme sacrifice of yourself in order to reveal the mystery of the Father's love and his plan of mercy and salvation for all peoples, we adore you and praise you, because you have enlightened and redeemed us.

O Jesus, you who sent out your apostles to gather in the harvest from all the fields of the world and did promise to draw all men to yourself on the cross, we thank you for having sent to us those who have taught us the truth and made us sharers in your grace.

Pope John XXIII, 1881–1963

✿ NOVEMBER 14 ✿

Enter my heart, O Holy Spirit,
   come in blessed mercy and set me free.
Throw open, O Lord, the locked doors of my mind;
   cleanse the chambers of my thought for thy dwelling:
   light there the fires of thine own holy brightness in new
      understandings of truth,
O Holy Spirit, very God, whose presence is liberty,
   grant me the perfect freedom
      to be thy servant
   today, tomorrow, evermore.

Eric Milner-White, 1884–1963

✿ NOVEMBER 15 ✿

From all my lame defeats and oh! much more
From all the victories that I seemed to score;
From cleverness shot forth on thy behalf,
At which, while angels weep, the audience laugh;
From all my proofs of thy divinity,
Thou, who wouldst give no sign, deliver me.

Thoughts are but coins. Let me not trust, instead
Of thee, their thin-worn image of thy head.
From all my thoughts, even from my thoughts of thee,
O thou fair silence, fall, and set me free.
Lord of the narrow gate and the needle's eye,
Take from me all my trumpery lest I die.

C.S. Lewis, 1898–1963

🌸 NOVEMBER 16 🌸

Father, we thank thee for our happiness: for thy great gift of life: for the
wonder and bloom of the world. We bless thee that it takes a very little
thing to make us happy, yet so great a thing to satisfy us that only thyself
canst do it, for thou alone art greater than our hearts. We bless thee for
thy calling which is so high that no man can perfectly attain unto it, and
for thy grace which stoops so low that none of us can ever fall too low
for it. Above all we bless thee that thou didst send thy Son, Jesus Christ
our Lord, for having seen him we have seen thee, whose truth doth ever
warm, and whose grace doth ever keep.

Helen Waddell, 1889–1965

🌸 NOVEMBER 17 🌸

Lord, give us grace
    to hold to thee
  when all is weariness and fear
  and sin abounds within, without
  when that which I would do I cannot do
  and that I do I would not do,
  when love itself is tested by the doubt
  that love is false, or dead within the soul,
  when every act brings new confusion, new distress,
      new opportunities, new misunderstandings,
  and every thought new accusation.

Lord, give us grace
    that we may know that in the darkness pressing round
    it is the mist of sin that hides thy face,
    that thou art there
    and thou dost know we love thee still…

Gilbert Shaw, 1886–1967

❈ NOVEMBER 18 ❈

O Lord our God, you know who we are; men with good consciences and with bad, persons who are content and those who are discontented, the certain and the uncertain, Christians by conviction and Christians by convention, those who believe and those who half-believe, those who disbelieve.

And you know where we have come from: from the circle of relatives, acquaintances and friends, or from the greatest loneliness; from a life of quiet prosperity, or from manifold confusion and distress; from family relationships that are well ordered or from those disordered, or under stress; from the inner circle of the Christian community or from its outer edge.

But now we all stand before you, in all our differences, yet alike in that we are all in the wrong with you and with one another, that we must all one day die, that we would be lost without your grace, but also in that your grace is promised and made available to us all in your dear Son, Jesus Christ.

Karl Barth, 1886–1968

❈ NOVEMBER 19 ❈

O God, save me from myself, save me from myself; this frivolous self which plays with your creation, this vain self which is clever about your creation, this masterful self which manipulates your creation, this greedy self which exploits your creation, this lazy self which soothes itself with your creation; this self which throws the thick shadow of its own purposes and desires in every direction in which I try to look, so that I cannot see what it is that you, my Lord and God, are showing to me. Teach me to stand out of my own light, and let your daylight shine.

Austin Farrer, 1904–68

🌂 NOVEMBER 20 🌂

My Lord God, I have no idea where I am going. I do not see the road ahead of me. I cannot know for certain where it will end. Nor do I really know myself, and the fact that I think I am following your will does not mean that I am actually doing so.

But I believe that the desire to please you does in fact please you, and I hope that I have that desire in all that I am doing. I hope that I never do anything apart from that desire. And I know that if I do this you will lead me by the right road though I may know nothing about it.

Therefore I will trust you always. Though I may seem to be lost and in the shadow of death I will not fear, for you are ever with me and you will never leave me to face my peril alone.

Thomas Merton, 1915–68

🌂 NOVEMBER 21 🌂

And now unto him who is able to keep us from falling and lift us from the dark valley of despair to the bright mountain of hope, from the midnight of desperation to the daybreak of joy; to him be power and authority, for ever and ever.

Martin Luther King, 1929–68

🌂 NOVEMBER 22 🌂

God, give us grace to accept with serenity
the things that cannot be changed,

courage to change the things that should be changed,
and the wisdom to distinguish the one from the other.

Reinhold Niebuhr, 1892–1971

🏵 NOVEMBER 23 🏵

O Lord God, who knowest our frame and rememberest that we are dust,
look in pity upon those who mourn. Make thy loving presence so real to
them that they may feel round about them thine everlasting arms,
upholding and strengthening them.

Grant them such a sense of certainty that their loved one is with
thee, doing thy high service, unhindered by pain, that they may turn to
life's tasks with brave hearts and steady nerves, consoled in the thought
that they will meet their dear one again.

Teach us all to face death unafraid and take us at last in triumph
through the shadows into thine everlasting light where are reunion and
never-ending joy. Through Jesus Christ our Lord.

Leslie D. Weatherhead, 1883–1975

🏵 NOVEMBER 24 🏵

O Father, give us the humility which
　Realizes its ignorance,
　Admits its mistakes,
　Recognizes its need,
　Welcomes advice,
　Accepts rebuke.
Help us always
　To praise rather than to criticize,
　To sympathize rather than to condemn.
　To encourage rather than to discourage,
　To build rather than to destroy,
　And to think of people at their best rather than at their worst.
This we ask for thy name's sake.

William Barclay, 1907–78

❧ NOVEMBER 25 ❧

What can I say to you, my God? Shall I collect together all the words that praise your holy name? Shall I give you all the names of this world, you, the Unnameable? Shall I call you 'God of my life, meaning of my existence, hallowing of my acts, my journey's end, bitterness of my bitter hours, home of my loneliness, you my most treasured happiness'? Shall I say: Creator, Sustainer, Pardoner, Near One, Distant One, Incomprehensible One, God both of flowers and stars, God of the gentle wind and of terrible battles, Wisdom, Power, Loyalty and Truthfulness, Eternity and Infinity, you the All-merciful, you the Just One, you Love itself?

Karl Rahner, 1904–84

❧ NOVEMBER 26 ❧

O Lord, open my eyes
that I may see the need of others,
open my ears that I may hear their cries,
open my heart so that they need not be without succour.
Let me not be afraid to defend the weak
because of the anger of the strong,
nor afraid to defend the poor
because of the anger of the rich.
Show me where love and hope and faith are needed,
and use me to bring them to these places.
Open my eyes and ears that I may, this coming day,
be able to do some work of peace for thee.

Alan Paton, 1903–88

❦ NOVEMBER 27 ❦

Almighty God, Creator:
In these last days storm has assailed us.
Greyness has enveloped and mist surrounded
our going out and our coming in.
Now again thy glory clarifies,
thy light lifts up our hearts to thee,
and night falls in peace.
But through mist and storm and sunshine,
the crops have ripened here
and vines of Spain have grown.
Thy constant care in all and everywhere is manifest.

Almighty God, Redeemer:
Even as with our bodies, so also with our souls.
Redeemer, Christ:
Sunshine and storm, mist and greyness
eddy round our inner lives.
But as we trace the pattern, looking back,
we know that both darkness and light have been of thine ordaining,
for our own soul's health
Thy constant care in all, and everywhere,
is manifest.

Almighty God, Sustainer:
Sun behind all suns,
Soul behind all souls,
everlasting reconciler of our whole beings:
Show to us in everything we touch and in everyone we meet
    the continued assurance of thy presence round us:
lest ever we should think thee absent.
In all created things thou art there.
In every friend we have
the sunshine of thy presence is shown forth.
In every enemy that seems to cross our path,
thou art there within the cloud
to challenge us to love.

Show to us the glory in the grey.
Awake for us thy presence in the very storm
till all our joys are seen as thee
and all our trivial tasks emerge as priestly sacraments
in the universal temple of thy love.

Of ourselves we cannot see this. Sure physician give us sight.
Of ourselves we cannot act. Patient love give us love:
till every shower of rain speaks of thy forgiveness:
till every move of light and shadow speaks of grave and resurrection:
to assure us that we cannot die:
thou creating, redeeming and sustaining God.

George Macleod, 1895–1991

🌸 NOVEMBER 28 🌸

Lord, increase my faith,
that I may embrace everything that is your will.
Lord, increase my faith
that the mountain of difficulty may be removed.
Lord, increase my faith that I may never be
at a loss for some creative action for you.
Lord, increase my faith that I may never be
impatient or frustrated.
Lord, increase my faith that I may run to you
in every situation.
Lord, increase my faith that I may trust you
in seeming failure or defeat.
Lord, increase my faith that I may endure
as seeing you who are visible only to the eye of faith.
Lord, fill me with faith, hope and love,
this day and always.

George Appleton, 1902–93

❧ NOVEMBER 29 ❧

Why, O Lord, is it so hard for me to keep my heart directed towards you? Why do the many little things I want to do, and the many people I know, keep crowding into my mind, even during the hours that I am totally free to be with you and you alone? Why does my mind wander off in so many directions, and why does my heart desire the things that lead me astray? Are you not enough for me? Do I keep doubting your love and care, your mercy and grace? Do I keep wondering, in the centre of my being, whether you will give me all I need if I just keep my eyes on you?

Please accept my distractions, my fatigue, my irritations, and my faithless wanderings. You know me more deeply and fully than I know myself. You love me with a greater love than I can love myself. You even offer me more than I can desire. Look at me, see me in all my misery and inner confusion, and let me sense your presence in the midst of my turmoil. All I can do is show myself to you. Yet, I am afraid to do so. I am afraid that you will reject me. But I know—with the knowledge of faith—that you desire to give me your love. The only thing you ask of me is not to hide from you, not to run away in despair, not to act as if you were a relentless despot.

Take my tired body, my confused mind, and my restless soul into your arms and give me rest, simple quiet rest. Do I ask too much too soon? I should not worry about that. You will let me know. Come, Lord Jesus, come. Amen.

Henri Nouwen, 1932–97

❧ NOVEMBER 30 ❧

Heavenly Father, we bring to you in prayer people who are suffering in mind or spirit.

We remember especially those facing long and incurable illness;
those cast down by the cares and sorrows of daily life;
those who have lost their faith and for whom the future is dark.

In your mercy maintain their courage, lift their burdens and renew their faith, that they may find in you their strength, their comfort and their peace, for our Saviour's sake.

Frank Colquhoun, 1909–97

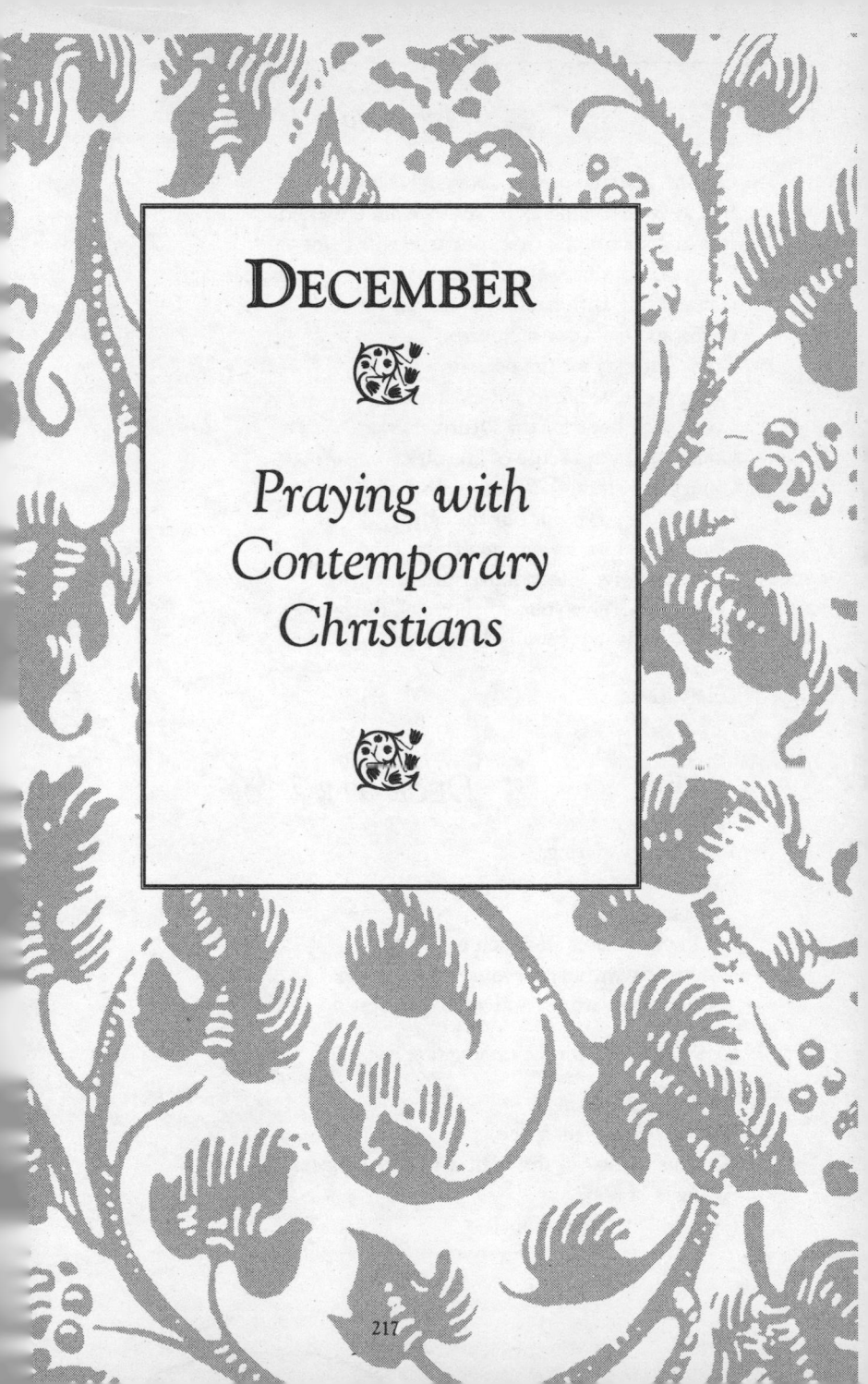

DECEMBER

Praying with
Contemporary
Christians

❦ DECEMBER 1 ❦

O Lord, give us yourself above all things.
It is in your coming alone that we are enriched.
It is in your coming that your true gifts come.
Come, Lord, that we may share the gifts of your presence.
Come, Lord, with healing of the past,
Come and calm our memories,
Come with joy for the present,
Come and give life to our existence,
Come with hope for the future,
Come and give a sense of eternity,
Come with strength for our wills,
Come with power for our thoughts,
Come with love for our heart,
Come and give affection to our being.
Come, Lord, give yourself above all things
And help us to give ourselves to you.

David Adam

❦ DECEMBER 2 ❦

You keep us waiting.
You, the God of all time;
Want us to wait
For the right time in which to discover
Who we are, where we must go,
Who will be with us, and what we must do.

So, thank you... for the waiting time.

You keep us looking.
You, the God of all space,
Want us to look in the right and wrong places
For signs of hope,
For people who are hopeless,

For visions of a better world which will appear
Among the disappointments of the world we know.

So, thank you... for the looking time.

You keep us loving.
You, the God whose name is love,
Want us to be like you—
To love the loveless and the unlovely and the unlovable;
To love without jealousy or design or threat;
And, most difficult of all,
To love ourselves.

So, thank you... for the loving time.

And in all this,
You keep us.
Through hard questions with no easy answers;
Through failing where we hoped to succeed
   and making an impact when we felt we were useless;
Through the patience and the dreams and the love of others;
And through Jesus Christ and his Spirit,
You
Keep us.

So, thank you... for the keeping time.
      And for now,
      and for ever.

John Bell

❀ DECEMBER 3 ❀

Help me, O God, to put off all pretences and to find my true self.
Help me, O God, to discard all false pictures of you, whatever the cost
to my comfort.
Help me, O God, to let go all my problems, and fix my mind on you.
Help me, O God, to see my own sins, never to judge my neighbour, and
may the glory be all yours.

Into your hands I commend my spirit.
Your will, not mine, be done.

Anthony Bloom

🕮 DECEMBER 4 🕮

Lord,
isn't your creation wasteful?
Fruits never equal
the seedlings' abundance.
Springs scatter water.
The sun gives out
enormous light.
May your bounty teach me
greatness of heart.
May your magnificence
Stop me being mean.
Seeing you a prodigal
and open-handed giver
let me give unstintingly
like a king's son
like God's own.

Helder Camara

🕮 DECEMBER 5 🕮

Lord of the Universe, Master of All,
look in love upon your people
Pour the healing oil of your compassion
on a world that is wounded and dying.
Send us out in search of the lost,
to comfort the afflicted,
to bind up the broken,
and to free those trapped
under the rubble of their fallen dreams.

Sheila Cassidy

❄ DECEMBER 6 ❄

Eternal Spirit,
Life-Giver, Pain-Bearer, Love-Maker,
Source of all that is and that shall be,
Father and Mother of us all,
Loving God, in whom is heaven:

The Hallowing of your Name
    echo through the universe!
The Way of your Justice
    be followed by the people of the world!
Your Heavenly Will
    be done by all created beings!
Your Commonwealth of Peace and Freedom
    sustain our hope and come on earth!

With the bread we need for today,
    feed us.
In the hurts we absorb from one another,
    forgive us.
In times of temptation and test,
    strengthen us.
From trials too great to endure,
    spare us.
From the grip of all that is evil,
    free us.

For you reign in the glory
    of the power that is love,
    now and for ever.

Jim Cotter

❄ DECEMBER 7 ❄

You big, bright, beautiful God,
this is my day for flying!
I reach out to the bigness of you.
I touch the brightness of you

and I feel the beauty of you
in the centre of my living.
Today you bear me up, up,
past my doubts about both of us,
to the certainty of your love.
Today, God, I know you.
All those words I learned
are burnt up in your fire,
You are sun to my Icarus,
candle to my moth.
Today I fly
and am dissolved in you!

And if tomorrow I am grounded
by a weight of anxieties,
if my feet are heavy and there are clouds
between me and the sun,
then let me keep hold of the warm place in my heart
reminding me that today I flew
and was kissed by God.

Joy Cowley

❧ DECEMBER 8 ❧

The story, Lord, is as old as history,
    as remorseless as man:
Man the raider, the plunderer, the terrorist,
    the conqueror,
Defiling the light of dawn with
The conspiracies of night,
Perverting to evil the fine instruments of nature,
Dealing fear among the tents and the homesteads
Of the unsuspecting or the weak,
Confiscating, purloining, devastating.

The passions are more subtle in our time—
The fire-power of bombs for the dust-clouds of cavalry,
Napalm and incendiary and machines in the skies,
Devices for war decrying the stars,
New skills with the same curse of destruction,
The sanctity of mankind in the jeopardy of techniques,
Gracelessness against the majesty on high.

By the truth of the eternal exposure,
By the reckoning of the eternal justice,
By compassion upon kin and kind,
By the awe of thy sovereignty,
Turn our deeds, O good Lord,
Repair our ravages,
Forgive our perversities.
O God, give peace, grateful peace.

Kenneth Cragg

🌺 DECEMBER 9 🌺

O my Lord, I discern in my anger a sense of self-righteousness which is much too close to pleasure. And I think of you, Lord. You were never angry in your own defence, and you took no pleasure in anger: else why the Cross? But you were angry for God: you were angry with those who sold him as a commodity; you were angry with those who used him for their own status; or who treated him as belonging only to them.

O Lord, implant in me a holy fear of the wrong kind of anger, which ministers to my own sense of self-importance, or is simply an indulgence of my own frustration. Forgive me, Lord, for all such occasions.

Ruth Etchells

❈ DECEMBER 10 ❈

Dear God, it is so hard for us not to be anxious.
We worry about work and money,
    about food and health,
    about weather and crops,
    about war and politics
    about loving and being loved.
Show us how perfect love casts out fear.

Monica Furlong

❈ DECEMBER 11 ❈

Our brother Jesus, you set our feet upon the way and sometimes
    where you lead we do not like or understand.
Bless us with courage where the way is fraught with dread or danger;
Bless us with graceful meetings where the way is lonely;
Bless us with good companions where the way demands a common
    cause;
Bless us with night vision where we travel in the dark, keen hearing
    where we have not sight, to hear the reassuring sounds of fellow
    travellers,
Bless us with humour—we cannot travel lightly weighed down with
    gravity;
Bless us with humility to learn from those around us;
Bless us with decisiveness where we must move with speed;
Bless us with lazy moments, to stretch and rest and savour;
Bless us with love, given and received;
And bless us with your presence, even when we know it in your
    absence.
Lead us into exile,
until we find that on the road
    is where you are,
and where you are is going home.
Bless us, lead us, love us, bring us home
    bearing the gospel of life.

Kathy Galloway

Lord, I'm tired of being ill all the time, sick of minor but exhausting ailments and sick of feeling weak after every effort to accomplish something.

I am tired of hearing people say: 'There is always something wrong with…'

True, there *is* always something wrong with me. Nothing serious, nothing which makes others look at me and sadly think: 'It could happen to me…'

Not even that. What happens to me is of no great consequence. Minor little illnesses which don't scare anyone: a headache here and a cold there; then something wrong with my stomach, and then something else again. Little nothings.

But there is no end to it. And my patience is running out.

I'm beginning to dream about another life, a life without illness. A strong and healthy life where I get up fresh and rested every morning, ready to meet everything with a smile. A beautiful life: the product of my imagination.

And then I begin to envy people. The healthy ones. I think it's unjust: their relaxed expression, their fresh complexion, their meals without fears and worries. And that smile they put on when they say to me: 'So, what's wrong with you today?' as if they knew what illness was all about.

Forgive me, Lord, for having been unjust. I know that it isn't altogether my fault. But I was nevertheless angry with them. That's stupid.

Teach me, Lord, to understand—that they don't understand.

When I don't feel like doing a thing, give me strength. Strength not to give in, as they say. Strength to try at any rate.

Lord, help me to bear my endless little miseries with some flair.

Paul Geres

❧ DECEMBER 13 ❧

O come, Holy Spirit, inflame my heart, set it on fire with love. Burn away my self-centredness so that I can love unselfishly. Breathe your life-giving breath into my soul so that I can live freely and joyously, unrestricted by self-consciousness, and may be ready to go wherever you may send me. Come like a gentle breeze and give me your still peace so that I may be quiet and know the wonder of your presence, and help diffuse it in the world. Never let me shut you out; never let me try to limit you to my capacity; act freely in me and through me, never leave me, O Lord and giver of life!

Michael Hollings and Etta Gullick

❧ DECEMBER 14 ❧

Let the healing grace of your love, O Lord, so transform me that I may play my part in the transfiguration of the world from a place of suffering, death and corruption to a realm of infinite light, joy and love. Make me so obedient to your Spirit that my life may become a living prayer, and a witness to your unfailing presence.

Martin Israel

❧ DECEMBER 15 ❧

To you, Creator of nature and humanity, of truth and beauty, I pray:

Hear my voice, for it is the voice of the victims of all wars and violence among individuals and nations.

Hear my voice, for it is the voice of all children who suffer and will suffer when people put their faith in weapons and war.

Hear my voice when I beg you to instil into the hearts of all human beings the wisdom of peace, the strength of justice and the joy of fellowship.

Hear my voice and grant insight and strength so that we may always respond to hatred with love, to injustice with total dedication to justice, to need with the sharing of self, to war with peace.

O God, hear my voice, and grant unto the world your everlasting peace.

Pope John Paul II

🏵 DECEMBER 16 🏵

God help us to find our confession,
The truth within us which is hidden from our mind,
The beauty or the ugliness we see elsewhere
But never in ourselves;
The stowaway which has been smuggled
Into the dark side of the heart,
Which puts the heart off balance and causes it pain,
Which wearies and confuses us,
Which tips us in false directions and inclines us to destruction,
The load which is not carried squarely
Because it is carried in ignorance
God help us to find our confession.
Help us across the boundary of our understanding.
Lead us into the darkness that we may find what lies concealed.
That we may confess it towards the light,
That we carry our truth in the centre of our heart;
That we may carry our cross wisely
And bring harmony into our life and our world.

Michael Leunig

🏵 DECEMBER 17 🏵

O Jesus, King of the poor,
shield this night
those who are imprisoned without charge,
those who have 'disappeared'.
Cast a halo of your presence around those
who groan in sorrow or pain.

Protect those whose livelihoods are threatened.
Encourage those forbidden to worship.
Encompass your little ones
gone hungry to sleep,
cold and fitfully waking.
Guide your witnesses for peace.
Safeguard your workers for justice.

Encircle us with your power,
Compass us with your grace,
embrace your dying ones,
support your weary ones,
calm your frightened ones—

and as the sun scatters the mist on the hills,
bring us to a new dawn,
when all shall freely
sit at table in your kingdom,
rejoicing in a God who makes all things new.

Kate McIlhagga

❧ DECEMBER 18 ❧

God the Father, God beyond us, we adore you.
   You are the depth of all that is.
   You are the ground of our being.
   We can never grasp you, yet you grasp us;
   the universe speaks of you to us, and your love comes to us through
      Jesus.
God the Son, God beside us, we adore you.
   You are the perfection of humanity.
   You have shown us what human life should be like.
   In you we see divine love and human greatness combined.
God the Spirit, God around us, we adore you.
   You draw us to Jesus and the Father.
   You are power within us.

You give us abundant life and can make us the men and women we
    are meant to be.
Father, Son and Spirit;
God, beyond, beside and around us;
We adore you.

Caryl Micklem

❦ DECEMBER 19 ❦

O God, Giver of Life, Bearer of Pain, Maker of Love,
    you are able to accept in us what we cannot even acknowledge:
    you are able to name in us what we cannot bear to speak of;
    you are able to hold in your memory what we have tried to forget;
    you are able to hold out to us the glory that we cannot conceive of.
    Reconcile us through your cross to all that we have rejected in our
selves, that we may find no part of your creation to be alien or strange
to us, and that we ourselves may be made whole. Through Jesus Christ,
our lover and our friend.

Janet Morley

❦ DECEMBER 20 ❦

God of the high and holy places
where I catch a glimpse of your glory,
above the low levels of life,
above the evil and emptiness which drags me down,
beyond the limits of my senses and imagination,
You lift me up.

In the splendour of a sunset,
in the silence of the stars,
in the grandeur of the mountains,
in the vastness of the sea,
You lift me up.

In the majesty of music,
in the mystery of art,
in the freshness of the morning,
in the fragrance of a single flower,
You lift me up.

Awe-inspiring God,
when I am lost in wonder
and lost for words,
receive the homage of my silent worship
but do not let me be content to bear your beauty and be still.
Go with me to the places where I live and work.
Lift the veil of reticence behind which I hide.
Give me the courage to speak of the things which move me,
with simple and unselfconscious delight.
Help me to share my glimpses of glory
until others are drawn to your light.

Jean Mortimer

🕮 DECEMBER 21 🕮

Let us pray for all those, throughout the world, who believe in the
    Gospel:
That they may grow in grace and humanity.
Let us also pray for all churches, that they may not lay up treasures on
    earth or become monuments to a past age,
Clinging to what is already dead and remote from people of today,
But that they may be converted and receive the spirit of Jesus, our Lord,
    who is the light and life, hope and peace of this world, for ever and ever.

Huub Oosterhuis

Lord, here we are,
   out of breath,
   out of courage,
   and almost out of hope.
Caught between the infinity of our desires
   and the limitations of our means,
      we're tossed about,
      torn,
      pulled here and pulled there,
      confused,
      and exhausted.
So, Lord, here we are,
      finally still,
      and finally ready to listen.

You've seen how our dissatisfaction has made us suffer.
You've seen how fear has led us astray in choosing our commitments.
You've seen how we were afraid of doing too little.
And you've seen the cross imposed by our limited means.

Lord, make us strong enough to do what we should do
     calmly,
     simply,
     without wanting to do too much,
     without wanting to do it all ourselves.
In other words, Lord, make us humble
     in our wish and our will to serve.
Help us above all to find you in our commitments,
   For you are the unity of our actions;
     You are the single love
       in all our loves,
       in all our efforts.
You are the well spring,
And all things are drawn to you.
So, we have come before you, Lord,
   to rest and gather our strength.

Michel Quoist

❧ DECEMBER 23 ❧

O Christ,
tirelessly you seek out those who are looking for you
and who think that you are far away;
teach us, at every moment,
to place our spirits in your hands.
While we are still looking for you,
already you have found us.
However poor our prayer,
you hear us far more than we can imagine or believe.

Brother Roger of Taizé

❧ DECEMBER 24 ❧

O God, it is easy to love the whole world, but hard to love the person
one works next to;
O God, it is easy to campaign for world peace, but hard to contribute
to the peace within my own home;
O God, it is easy to be fascinated with some new truth, and miss you in
the thing I have known so long;
O God, it is easy to share my home and possessions with people I like.
Teach me how to be generous towards others.
Enable me today to say something, or do something that will make a
difference to the discouraged, to the inexperienced, to the despairing.
Let no selfish concern with my own affairs shut me off from any today.
For your love's sake.

Rita Snowden

❧ DECEMBER 25 ❧

How easy, Lord, it is for me to live with you.
How easy it is for me to believe in you.
When my understanding is perplexed by doubts
or on the point of giving up,
when the most intelligent men see no further
than the coming evening, and know not
what they shall do tomorrow,
you send me a clear assurance
that you are there and that you will ensure
that not all the roads of goodness are barred.

From the heights of earthly fame I look back
in wonder at the road that led
through hopelessness
to this place whence I can send
mankind a reflection of your radiance.

And whatever I in this life may yet reflect,
that you will give me;
And whatever I shall not attain,
that, plainly, you have purposed for others.

Alexander Solzhenitsyn

❧ DECEMBER 26 ❧

Our heavenly Father, we commend to your mercy those for whom life
does not spell freedom: prisoners of conscience, the homeless and the
handicapped, the sick in body and mind, the elderly who are confined to
their homes, those who are enslaved by their passions, and those who
are addicted to drugs. Grant that, whatever their outward
circumstances, they may find inward freedom, through him who
proclaimed release to captives, Jesus Christ our Saviour.

John R.W. Stott

❦ DECEMBER 27 ❧

Lord Jesus Christ,
alive and at large in the world,
help me to follow and find you there today,
in the places where I work,
meet people,
spend money,
and make plans.
Take me as a disciple of your kingdom,
to see through your eyes,
and hear the questions you are asking,
to welcome all others with your trust and truth,
and to change the things that contradict God's love,
by the power of the cross
and the freedom of your Spirit.

John V. Taylor

❦ DECEMBER 28 ❧

Lord, your harvest is the harvest of love;
love sown in the hearts of people;
love that spreads out
like the branches of a great tree
covering all who seek its shelter;
love that inspires and recreates;
love that is planted in the weak and the weary,
the sick and the dying.
The harvest of your love is the life that reaches
through the weeds of sin and death
to the sunlight of resurrection.
Lord, nurture my days with your love,
water my soul with the dew of forgiveness,
that the harvest of my life might be your joy.

Frank Topping

❄ DECEMBER 29 ❄

Bless our beautiful land, O Lord,
with its wonderful variety of people,
of races, cultures and languages.
May we be a nation
of laughter and joy,
of justice and reconciliation,
of peace and unity,
of compassion, caring and sharing.
We pray this prayer for a true patriotism,
in the powerful name of Jesus our Lord.

Desmond Tutu

❄ DECEMBER 30 ❄

O Lord:

In a world where many are lonely:
We thank you for our friendships.

In a world where many are captive:
We thank you for our freedom.

In a world where many are hungry:
We thank you for your provision.

We pray that you will:
Enlarge our sympathy,
Deepen our compassion,
And give us grateful hearts.
In Christ's name.

Terry Waite

Creator of Earth
and of all earth's children,
Creator of soil and sea and sky
and the tapestries of stars,
we turn to you for guidance
as we look on our mutilated planet,
and pray it is not too late for us
to rescue our wounded world.
We have been so careless.
We have failed to nurture the fragile life
You entrusted to our keeping.
We beg you for forgiveness
and we ask you to begin again.
Be with us in our commitment to earth.
Let all the earth say: Amen.

Miriam Therese Winter

INDEX OF SOURCES

Cotton, George   Sep 8
Coverdale, Miles   Aug 10
Cowley, Joy   Dec 7
Cowper, William   Jul 11
Cragg, Kenneth   Dec 8
Cranmer, Thomas   Aug 5
Crashaw, Richard   Jul 5
Cromwell, Oliver   Aug 17
Crossman, Samuel   Oct 1
Cummings, E.E.   Jul 26
Cyprian of Carthage   Mar 12

D

da Siena, Bianco   May 26
de Foucauld, Charles   Sep 27
de Sales, Francis   Jun 28
Dickinson, Emily   Jul 15
Didache, The   Mar 4
Dimitrii of Rostov   Jun 27
Dionysius of Alexandria   Mar 13
Donne, John   Jul 2
Drake, Sir Francis   Aug 14
Dream of the Rood, The   May 1
Dryden, John   Jul 8

E

Edmeston, James   Oct 11
Edmund of Abingdon   Jun 13
Eliot, T.S.   Jul 27
Elizabeth of the Trinity   May 12
Ellerton, John   Oct 19
Elliott, Charlotte   Oct 12
Ephraem of Syria   Mar 20
Erasmus   May 30
Erigena, Johannes Scotus   May 5

Etchells, Ruth   Dec 9
Eusebius   Mar 7

F

Farrer, Austin   Nov 19
Francis of Assisi   Jun 12
Francis, Prayer of St   Nov 1
Furlong, Monica   Dec 10

G

Galloway, Kathy   Dec 11
Gelasian Sacramentary, The   Mar 25
Geres, Paul   Dec 12
Gertrude the Great   Jun 19
Gilbert of Hoyland   May 11
Grant, Robert   Oct 8
Greek Liturgy   Mar 8
Green, Fred Pratt   Oct 31
Gregorian Sacramentary   Mar 28
Gregory I (Pope)   Jun 5
Gregory of Narek   May 8
Gregory of Nazianzus   Mar 22
Guigo the Carthusian   May 13
Gullick, Etta   Dec 13

H

Hadewijch of Brabant   May 14
Hammarskjold, Dag   Nov 12
Hatch, Edwin   Oct 17
Havergal, Frances Ridley   Oct 15
Henry, Matthew   Aug 21
Herbert, George   Jul 3
Herrick, Robert   Jul 6
Hilary of Poitiers   Mar 19

Hildegard of Bingen   Jun 11

Hilton, Walter   May 24

Hippolytus of Rome   Mar 10

Hollings, Michael   Dec 13

Hopkins, Gerard Manley   Jul 17

Hort, Fenton John Anthony   Sep 16

How, W.W.   Oct 21

Hoyland, John S.   Nov 9

Hunter, John   Sep 28

I

Irenaeus of Lyons   Mar 3

Israel, Martin   Dec 14

J

Jarrett, Bede   Nov 2

'Jesus Prayer, The'   May 9

Jewel, John   Aug 11

John, Father, of the Russian Church
   Sep 23

John of the Cross   Jun 26

John Paul II (Pope)   Dec 15

John XXIII (Pope)   Nov 13

Jonson, Ben   Jul 4

Jowett, J.H.   Aug 30

Julian of Norwich   May 25

K

Kagawa, Toyohiko   Nov 11

Keble, John   Oct 10

Ken, Thomas   Oct 2

Kierkegaard, Søren   Sep 7

King, Edward   Sep 24

King, Martin Luther   Nov 21

Kingsley, Charles   Sep 11

Kipling, Rudyard   Jul 25

Knox, John   Aug 12

L

L'Engle, Madeleine   Jul 31

Lawrence, D.H.   Jul 24

Leunig, Michael   Dec 16

Lewis, C.S.   Nov 15

Liturgy of Dunkeld   Apr 27

Liturgy of St Basil   Mar 15

Liturgy of St Dionysius   May 3

Liturgy of St James   Mar 5

Liturgy of St Mark   Mar 6

Longfellow, Henry Wadsworth   Jul 14

Loyola, Ignatius   Jun 24

Lull, Raymond   May 18

Luther, Martin   Aug 3

Lyte, Henry Francis   Oct 9

M

Macarius of Egypt   Mar 23

MacDonald, George   Sep 22

McIlhagga, Kate   Dec 17

Macleod, George   Nov 27

Macrina   Mar 16

Martin, Hugh   Oct 28

Masefield, John   Jul 28

Matheson, George   Oct 23

Mechthild of Magdeburg   Jun 18

Melanchthon, Philip   Aug 6

Merton, Thomas   Nov 20

Meuin   May 2

Meynell, Alice   Jul 22

Micklem, Caryl   Dec 18

Milner-White, Eric   Nov 14

Symeon the New Theologian   Jun 7

Synesius   Jun 3

T

Tadhg Og O Huiginn   Apr 23

Taylor, John V.   Dec 27

Te Deum   Mar 18

Temple, William   Nov 4

Tennyson, Alfred (Lord)   Jul 18

Teresa of Avila   Jun 25

Tersteegen, Gerhard   Oct 4

Thérèse of Lisieux   Jun 30

Thomas à Kempis   May 27

Thomas, R.S.   Jul 30

Topping, Frank   Dec 28

Tutu, Desmond   Dec 29

Twells, Henry   Oct 22

U

Underhill, Evelyn   Nov 3

V

Vaughan, Charles   Sep 18

Vaughan, Henry   Jul 7

Very, Jones   Jul 13

Vianney, Jean-Baptiste   Jun 29

Vives, Ludovicus   May 31

W

Waddell, Helen   Nov 16

Waite, Terry   Dec 30

Watt, Lauchlan Maclean   Nov 8

Watts, Isaac   Oct 3

Weatherhead, Leslie D.   Nov 23

Wells, H.G.   Nov 6

Wesley, Charles   Oct 5

Wesley, John   Aug 25

Wesley, Susanna   Aug 23

Westcott, Brooke Foss   Sep 20

Whitman, Walt   Jul 19

Whittier, John Greenleaf   Oct 18

Wilde, Oscar   Jul 21

William of Saint Thierry   May 10

Willis, Maria   Oct 25

Winslow, Jack C.   Oct 29

Winter, Miriam Therese   Dec 31

Woolman, John   Aug 24

X

Xavier, Francis   Jun 23

INDEX OF THEMES

dedication to God *continued*

Jun 10, 19, 21, 25, Aug 28, Sep 27, 30, Oct 14, 15, 16, 17, 23, 29, Nov 12

deliverance *see* salvation

departed, the   Sep 16

desire   Apr 2,

for God *see* longing for God

despair *see* hope

distractions   Apr 8, Nov 29

doubt, doubts   Jul 26, Sep 6, 21, Nov 29, Dec 25

E

earth *see* creation

endurance *see* perseverence

envy   Jan 11, 18, Dec 12

evil   Jan 11, 29, Feb 11, 14, Jul 16; *see also* wicked, wickedness

F

faith   Feb 12, Mar 14, 19, Apr 11, Jun 8, Jul 18, Aug 3, 9, Sep 6, 21, Oct 31, Nov 28, 30

family   Sep 17, Oct 26, 28

fear   Jul 2

finishing   Aug 14

forgive, forgiveness   Jan 9, 23, Feb 11, Mar 23, Apr 6, Jul 2, 23, Aug 2, Oct 11

freedom   Dec 26

friends, absent   Mar 7, Sep 26

future   Aug 13, Sep 2, 12, Nov 20, 30

G

generosity   Jun 24, Dec 4

God

all-seeing   Jan 28, Mar 14, May 8

God *continued*

anger of   Jan 20, Feb 3, 8, 9

attributes of   Jun 7

creator   Jan 1, 5, Mar 10, 30, Apr 11, 17, 23, Jun 17, 24, 28, 31, Jul 17, 18, 19, 27, Oct 8, Dec 31

everywhere   Jan 28, Sep 5, Oct 13

fatherhood of   Jan 23, Feb 9, 10, 11, Mar 9, Apr 11, Oct 13

glory of   Jan 5, 21, 30, Feb 2, 27, Jul 27, Oct 13, Nov 27, Dec 20; *see also* God, greatness of

goodness of   Jan 4, 10, 23, 30, Feb 5, Mar 4, 6, Apr 18, Jun 2, 22, Jul 3, Aug 15, Sep 24, Oct 6, 27

grace of   Apr 24, Aug 21, Oct 7, Nov 13, 16, 18; *see also* God, goodness of

greatness of   Jan 1, 9, 20, 21, 24, 25, 28, 30, Feb 2, 17, 28, Apr 20, May 13, Oct 6, 24

guidance of   Jan 4, 7, May 6, 30, Jun 3, 17, Jul 6, 14, 22, Aug 6, Sep 7, 9, 13, 25, Oct 11 ,14, 16, Dec 31

hiddenness of   Jan 2, 6, Feb 9, Apr 1, May 23, Aug 24, Sep 7, Oct 24, Nov 17

image of   Jun 9, Aug 30

in us   Feb 18, May 15, 24, Jun 11, Sep 5, 12, 15, Nov 11

judgement of   Jan 2, 21, 23, Feb 13, Jul 15, Nov 18

kingdom of   Jan 30, Feb 2, 11, 12, 23, Mar 12, Apr 17, 27, Jul 23, Sep 25, Oct 19, Nov 6

law of   Jan 5, 26

love of   Jan 8, 10, 13, 23, Feb 9, 26, Mar 4, May 10, 11, Jun 20, Jul 11, Aug 15, Oct 1, 5, 12, 21, Dec 28; *see also* Christ, sacrifice of

mercy of   Jan 9, 23, Feb 8, 13, Mar 5, May 2, 9, Jun 9,

our saviour   Feb 27

P

paradise   Mar 16, Jul 3

parents   Oct 28

patience   Jan 11, Jun 26, Aug 10, Sep 18, Nov 29, Dec 2; *see also* perseverence

peace (spiritual)   Jan 27, Feb 1, 22, Aug 8, Sep 9, 12, 25, Oct 18, Nov 5, 9

  between people   Jan 17, Mar 5, 13, Apr 25, May 3, 31, Nov 26, 1, Dec 8, 15, 29; *see also* reconcile, reconciliation; unity between nations

peaceableness   Mar 7

penitence   May 29, Jul 4, Nov 11; *see also* repentance

perseverance   Feb 23, Mar 12, Jun 14, Aug 14; *see also* patience

pleasures   Sep 24

poor, the *see* needy, the; oppressed, oppression

praise of God   Jan 21, 25, 30, 31, Feb 13, 28, Mar 26, Apr 5, 10, Jul 17, 25, Oct 8, 26, Nov 25; *see also* God, greatness of

prayer, prayers   Mar 14, Apr 15, Sep 1

  morning   Mar 8, Apr 13, May 21, Jun 5, Jul 26, Aug 31, Sep 9, 12, 13, Nov 5, Dec 24, 27

  evening   Mar 23, 31, Apr 7, 24, 28, Jun17, Aug 2, 8, 16, Sep 17, Oct 2, 9, 10 ,19, 22, Dec 17

preachers   Aug 12

pride, proud   Jan 18, 27, Feb 13

promises   Feb 4

purity of heart   Mar 15, 28, May 7, Aug 30, Nov 12

R

reconcile, reconciliation   Mar 13, Nov1, Dec 19

repentance   Apr 6, 30, May 29, Jun 30, Aug 9, Nov 8, 11; *see also* confession; penance

reputation   Nov 10

resentment   May 11

rest, in God   Jun 2, 3, Jul 10, Sep 16, Oct 4, Nov 9, 29

restless heart   Jun 2, Oct 4

resurrection   Mar 16; *see also* heaven

riches, futility of   Jan 14

rulers and government   Mar 2, Sep 3

S

sacrifice   Feb 14, Sep 10; *see also* unselfishness

salvation   Feb 23, Mar 5, 16, May 4, Jun 11, 30, Jul 24, Sep 22, 23, Oct 5, 7, Nov 13

seeking God   May 5, Jun 4, 7, 15, 27, Aug 20, Sep 8, Oct 4, Dec 23; *see also* longing for God

self-abandonment   Sep 27

self-control   Mar 7, 29, Apr 8, Jun 26, Aug 21

self-knowledge   Dec 3, 16

self-righteousness   Dec 9

self-will   Oct 4, 14

serenity   Nov 22

service *see* dedication to God

silence   Sep 7

sin, sins   Jan 9, 15, 20, Feb 9, 25, Mar 6, 20, 24, May 8, Jul 2, 4, 5, 6, Aug 2, 8, 25, 27, Nov 17

sleep   Jun 18

strength (spiritual)   Feb 18, 24, Mar 29, Apr 20, 27, May 13, 28, Jun 6, Aug 3, 26, Sep 14, Oct 25, Nov 8, Dec 1, 22

stress   Oct 18, 31; *see also* worry, worries

suffer, suffering   Jan 2, 8, 22, Feb 7, 25, Jul 29, Sep 22, Nov 30

sympathy *see* compassion

T

temptation *see* self-will; sin, sins; strength

thanksgiving   Mar 4, Apr 19, Sep 23, Dec 30

thoughts   Apr 8, Nov 7, Nov 15

time   Mar 30, Dec 2

travellers   Mar 25

Trinity *see* God the Trinity

trouble, troubles   Jan 2, 19, Mar 11, May 28, Jun 6, Jul 21, Aug 18; *see also* suffer, suffering; worry, worries

trust   Jan 8, 10, 11, 19, 27, Apr 1, Jun 2, 16, Aug 29, Oct 12, Nov 9, 20, Dec 25

truth   Sep 20

U

understanding   Feb 23, Jun 8, Aug 4, Nov 14

unity, Christian   Mar 5, 12, 13, May 3

between nations   Sep 8, Nov 6

unity, Christian *continued*

with Christ   Feb 22, May 22, Jun 28

unselfishness   Sep 10, 11, 28, Nov 10, Dec 13, 24

W

waiting   Jan 11, Nov 29, Dec 2; *see also* patience

war   Nov 11, Dec 8, 15

weakness   May 8, Jul 14, Oct 11, Oct 25, Nov 6

wealth, futility of   Jan 14

weariness   Jul 29, Nov 29

whole, wholeness   Apr 14, Dec 19

wicked, wickedness   Jan 2, 12, 18, 29 Mar 6

wisdom   Jan 20, 25, Feb 4, 17, 23, Jun 4, 13, 17, Aug 11, Sep 3, 4, Nov 22

work   Aug 26

worry, worries   Jan 8, Feb 12

worship *see* praise of God

ACKNOWLEDGMENTS

We would like to thank all those who have given us permission to include quotations in this book, as indicated in the list below. Every effort has been made to trace and acknowledge copyright holders of all the quotations included in this book. We apologize for any errors or omissions that may remain, and would ask those concerned to contact the publishers, who will ensure that full acknowledgment is made in the future.

Extract from *In His Name* by George Appleton, is reproduced by permission of The Lutterworth Press.

Prayer by John Bell, copyright © Iona Community, Glasgow G51 3UU, Scotland.

'O God, early in the morning I cry to you...' reprinted with the permission of Simon & Schuster from *Letters and Papers from Prison*, revised, enlarged edition by Dietrich Bonhoeffer, translated by Reginald Fuller, Frank Clark *et al*. Copyright © 1953, 1967, 1971 by SCM Press Ltd.

Extracts from *Carmina Gadelica*, collected by Alexander Carmichael, published by Scottish Academic Press, 1928.

'Lord of the Universe...' taken from *Good Friday People* by Sheila Cassidy published and copyright 1991 by Darton, Longman and Todd Ltd and used by permission of the publishers.

Extract by Columba from *Iona, Earliest Poetry of a Celtic Monastery* (p. 36), translated and edited by Gilbert Markus and Dr Thomas Clancy. Used by permission of Edinburgh University Press and Gilbert Markus, 1995.

'Eternal Spirit...' by Jim Cotter. Copyright © Jim Cotter. Reproduced by permission of the author.

'i thank You God for this most amazing...' is reprinted from *Complete Poems 1904–62* by E.E. Cummings, edited by George J. Firmage, by permission of W.W. Norton & Company Ltd. Copyright © 1991 by the Trustees for the E.E. Cummings Trust and George James Firmage.

'We praise Thee, O God, for Thy glory...' from *Murder in the Cathedral* by T.S. Eliot, reproduced by permission of Faber and Faber Ltd.

'Lord, I'm tired of being ill...' reprinted from *Prayers for Impossible Days* by Paul Geres, copyright © 1976 Fortress Press. Used by permission of Augsberg Fortress.

'Thou who art over us...' from *Markings* by Dag Hammarskjold, translated by Leif Sjoberg and W.H. Auden. Translation copyright © 1964 by Alfred A. Knopf Inc. and Faber and Faber Ltd. Reprinted by permission.

'O Lord my God! (How Great Thou Art!)' by Stuart K. Hine. Copyright © 1953 Stuart K. Hine/Kingsway's Thankyou Music, PO Box 75, Eastbourne, East Sussex, BN23 6NW, UK. Used by kind permission of Kingsway's Thankyou Music.

'The Hands of God' by D.H. Lawrence from *The Complete Poems of D.H. Lawrence*, edited by V. de Sola Pinto and F.W. Roberts.

BIBLE ACKNOWLEDGMENTS